GUTSY PIONEERS

From Bullock Teams to Boom Times

◆

RITA PAULOS

Gutsy Pioneers: From Bullock Teams to Boom Times
© Rita Paulos 2024

Published by Rita Paulos

www.ritapaulos.com

ISBN paperback: 978-1-7636220-0-5
ISBN ebook: 978-1-7636220-1-2

Design & typesetting: Beckon Creative

First edition published as *Reared In A Tent*, ebook, 2008
ISBN 978-1-4476317-5-0

 A catalogue record for this book is available from the National Library of Australia

By the same author:

Simple Steps to Success, 2019
ISBN paperback: 978-1-6847006-0-8
ISBN ebook: 978-1-6847009-4-3

GUTSY PIONEERS

From Bullock Teams to Boom Times

RITA PAULOS

CONTENTS

Foreword	i
Preface	iii
Acknowledgements	iv
About the Author	v
The Pioneering Years	1
1851–1937: Christian 'Christy' Carl Sophus Andersen	2
1849–1915: Hans Hansen (Carpenter)	3
1853–1916: John Russell (British Army)	3
1852–1916: David Myles (Snr)	4
My Context	7
Introduction to the Early Days	8
1855–1897: Cania Station/Clonmel/Yarrol	9
1914–192: World War I	9
1916–1976: Golden Plateau Cracow, Qld	10
Cracow Hospital	12
People on the Move	12
1900: Cania Mine	13
1900: Bullock Teams Replacing Horse Teams	13
1880–1919: Christian Andersen, Blacksmith	14
1891–1912: Monal Mine	17
1890: Monal Mine	19
1910: Monal Township	23

1845–1924: Many Peaks	28
1898–1910: Many Peaks Copper Mine	29
1920: Many Peaks Township	30
1907: Epidemics	33
1920: Vaccinations	34
1920–30s: Boyne Valley Railway Tunnels	35
1914–1920: Horse and Wagon Transport	36
1923: Dooboon	37
1924–2022: Monto	38
1927: Building the Silverwood Dam	44
1926–1969: The Transition Years	46
1920–1930s: Transition From Horse to Automobile	70
1930: Mt Mee Roadworks	74
1932: Depression	75
1939–1945: During the War	78
1942: Savills' Farm	79
Being Bored Makes for Mischief	87
Tough Times	88
Lights	91
Predators and Prey	92
Nuisances When Camping On Site	93
On the Spot Nursing Aid	94
Improvising and Flexibility for Cooling	95
1945: September 2nd Ended the War	98
1946: Howies' Farm	101
1946: Ludlows' Farm, Kalpowar	106

1948: Wash Day inventions	109
Land Clearing	111
1957–1958: A Tour of a Farmer's Dairy	119
Journey Through Education	122
1950: Our Own House Near the Tennis Court	131
1952–1953: St Faiths Boarding School, Yeppoon	141
1970s: The Modern Era	146
Glossary	148
Footnotes	152
Endnote	158

Foreword

Thanks to Rita who encouraged me to put into words the extended history for our grandmother and her Irish connections. This would not have happened without Rita encouraging, urging and actually pushing me to do this reflection.

I trust it has added to what Rita has already researched and written about the history of the early life of our ancestors.

Margaret List (Myles)

Preface

Just twelve years ago I wrote a small book, *Reared in a Tent*, to help share my childhood experiences with my children, grandchildren and other family members. Since the family has grown and increased in size, there are great-grandchildren to pass these stories onto. It seemed a worthy project. I have tried to add as many photos as possible, more to show and help explain how the times were in the pioneering days. Whilst I had some of the photos that were faded, I did try to access some of the vintage times on the internet. The quality of the photos are not always up to par since they are almost a century old. In the old times it was necessary to go to a professional photographer's studio to obtain good quality photos. On every Box Brownie photo there is a stamp on the back displaying the word *KODAK*. Thanks to Kodak for their technology, since a picture is worth a thousand words. In this day and age, the time of instant photos on phones, I have learned that not a lot of people have kept real stories to attach to photos they have found while gathering their loved ones' belongings. It is now that I wish I had taken more notice of the details when my folks were alive. As time has gone by and I talk about my childhood, I realise how unique it was compared to those people who lived in the city; and certainly, a far cry from today's style of living.

Rita Paulos

Acknowledgements

This book has been written with the input of my cousins and second cousins, and I name a few, and thank them for their interest. Donald Myles has helped heaps with finding old photographs that Verna Myles (RIP) had taken many years ago; Carol Watson for her patience when I was unable to find my saved copies; Margaret List who has a lot of stories from her childhood, and since her trip to Ireland seven years ago, has really got into researching part of our family beginnings; Ann Ludlow for doing what she could to find photos I needed; Kevin Curd has taken photos of old things that are on their property, or collected by their families over the years. Matthew Curd is an IT whiz and made using the editing software look easy. Thanks also to Chris Dewar who had edited the 'flow' of the content to help the reader identify who is who, and what was what, especially when I kept jumping from one generation to the other! Also, to Giuseppe Poli for his Photoshop skills and assistance with the photo enhancing.

Thanks heaps to all for the encouragement to keep me going when I felt overwhelmed trying to put things in their perspective.

Credits to: *Stone Chimneys* written by Max Walker, Monto Magic, Google, Queensland Places, *The Chronicle*, Wikipedia, National Library of Australia, Department of Mines, Queensland Bell Makers, and Trove for their well-kept records of the past history. It was so good to be able to validate my own stories, and particularly those stories attached to the photos the family had kept for many years.

About the Author

This book, *Gutsy Pioneers* follows on from *Reared in a Tent*, which is a about a country-bred girl who was reared following the 1932 Depression and prior to the 1939/45 War. It was survival to some extent in Queensland, Australia.

I, Rita May Hansen, was born on 15 March 1938 at Cracow, Queensland during the Gold Rush. I was the first girl born at the Cracow Hospital — what a gem!

This reflection on my life, and that of my ancestors, has taken me back a long way in history. I have never really pondered over my childhood but rather used the resources to enrich my life.

There has been an enormous change over the last eighty years. Higher living standards, brought about by the ability to have confidence in using the bank credit facilities, not to forget what advanced technology has done to our education system, our working environment, our children's use of their spare time, and the reliance on computers, mobile phones, and particularly Google, Wikipedia and YouTube to provide answers for so many things.

The Pioneering Years

My story focuses around two families from the pioneering times, Hansen/Andersen on my dad's side and Myles/Russell on my mother's side. Both families had arrived by boat from their birth country and suffered the same loss of young children due to the close living conditions and epidemics that were prevalent in those days.

In fact, as you keep reading, you might think that they should have turned back. No doubt there were reasons hard to understand, and they were determined to have a fresh start in a new country.

1851–1937
Christian 'Christy'
Carl Sophus Andersen

Christy was my great grandfather, my dad Stefan (Tib) Hansen's grandfather. Christy was born on 3rd January, 1851, at Odense in Denmark. He passed away in 1937. He became a blacksmith and rail smith and was declared to be an upright journeyman by five fellow tradesmen who signed his certificate when he was nineteen years old. Christy, with his parents (Peter Steffan Andersen/Hedevig Larsen), his four brothers and three sisters (Hans, Christian, Peter, Christina, Annie, Karen, Neils), left Hamburg, Germany, on the sailing ship *Friedeberg* on April 20, 1871 for Brisbane.

They had migrated to Zillmere, Brisbane, living in migrant huts at "Zillman Waterholes". They were upset that the accommodation was worse than the pigs lived back in Denmark.

The family moved to Caboolture in 1876. Peter built a stone house on land now known as Henzell's paddock; farmed, with only partial success. Hedevig and the three girls raised silk worms and spun the silk on spinning wheels in a work room at the house where they made silk lace. The lace was sent to England as a gift from the Qld Government to commemorate Queen Victoria's Golden Jubilee. Later in time banana ripening rooms were built where the house once stood.

Christy, as a young man of twenty-five, made his way west to the Darling Downs in 1876. Very early in this period he worked as a blacksmith at Chinchilla, as well as in the construction of the Western Line between Dalby and Miles for two years.

Christy married Louise Franziska Fechner at the residence of the Lutheran Minister in Toowoomba in 1877; they lived in Dalby and then moved to Miles in 1878 where he bought a block of land at the corner of Marian and Tully Streets and set up a Smithy. Christie and Franziska had 6 sons and 4 daughters. He also erected a sawmill at Paddy's Creek, 5 miles west of Miles about this time. Christy was naturalised in Dalby in 1881. In 1888 he selected leasehold properties including "Christiansburg" to graze horses. During his stay at Christiansburg (1883/1905) he employed many men. The Andersen family suffered great sadness of losing their first born, Franz Christian, as a young man in an accident at the sawmill.

Christie Andersen built the Union Hotel in 1902; he was a staunch labour follower. This hotel burnt down in 1947.

Christie lived in the Miles area for a total of 42 years before settling in Beaufort Street, Alderley. His wife Louise passed away in 1925 and Christie in 1937 aged 86.

Their third child, Bertha Muriel Louisa married Harry Hansen (father and mother of my dad) and they had seven children. 1907 was a horrendous year for this family when the 2 eldest girls died from diphtheria (Florrie May, Ivy Christiana), survived by Henry (Chook), born 1905 who was 9 months in hospital and survived diphtheria, then Stefan (Tib) (later anglicised to Stephen— my father was born in 1907,) followed by Arthur (Art) born 1910, Anne Mabel (May) born 1912, and Donald born 1920.

1849—1915
Hans Hansen
Carpenter

Hans came to Qld in 1872, sailed from Hamburg on the "Reichstag". Hans married Christina Julianne Andersen in 1876 when she was 18 years old. She passed away in 1954 aged 96 years. They had seven children, four boys and three girls, named Hedvi Elvera (Elsie), Henry Peter Christian (Dad's grandfather), Carl Frederick Stafeen , Annie Rasmine, Ruby May, William Norman, Laurence Stanley. The following gives a brief history of where the family dispersed to:

Hedvi (Elsie), Henry (Carpenter) and Bertha settled at Glasshouse Mountains on a pineapple farm. The Great Depression and drought of the 1930's, threw their life into disarray. They subsequently settled at Cracow; Carl Frederick, Anne Rasmine settled at Tingoora, Ruby May and James at Kilcoy, William Norman and Elsie at Moorooka, Laurence (Cabinet Maker) and Olive settled at Alderley and later retired to Redcliffe.

1853–1916
JOHN RUSSELL
British Army

John Russell and Isabella Myles (Muldrew) 1860/1945 and their family of two girls and one boy (Mary, Georgina and William), emigrated from Armah, Ireland, and settled at an area known as Three Mile Creek only 3km from Ipswich, in 1889. A further eight children, namely Jack, Claude, George, Colin, Stan, Lucinda, Jim and Amanda, were born in Qld. Subsequently, in the 1940's, the area where they settled was called Amberley by James and Martha Collett. Incidentally, Mary Russell's father John Russell was in the British Army.

1852–1916
DAVID MYLES (SNR)

1855–1943
CATHERINE ANGUS SCOTT

David Myles (Snr) and Catherine Angus Scott emigrated from Brechin, Scotland, and arrived in Brisbane about 1887, with the intention to teach new settlers how to build and store haystacks. He was known as a Pioneering Teamster. David & Catherine had 8 children; Sarah died from diphtheria on the ship coming to Brisbane and Mary died while they were in quarantine and is buried in the Paddington Cemetery. David Charles (Jnr) 'Stumpy' Myles was six years of age on arrival at Peach Tree Experimental Station. Subsequently, the whole family got work at the Monal mine. After David Snr passed in 1916 Catherine went to live at Littlemore, and much later moved to live with her son Ted Myles, who owned a property in close proximity to David Charles (Jnr). Catherine died in 1943 and is buried at the Monto Cemetery. David (Snr) and Catherine were my mother's grandparents.

Here is a copy of Catherine's impression of their arrival in Brisbane as told by her grand-daughter Catherine (Cass) Gassman:

> *Mr McCord nominated them out from Scotland.*
>
> *Dave, Jack and one sister (Mabel) were born in Scotland. Sarah and Mary got Diphtheria (one died on the way out from Scotland), the other is buried at the Paddington Cemetery in Brisbane (Lang Park).*
>
> *The family, and others, were quarantined in Brisbane under Government regulations for six weeks after arrival — "CONTAGIOUS DISEASE".*
>
> *When they had the OK to leave Brisbane a convoy of 6 or 7 drays and drivers turned up to take them, and off they went along a bush track. Granny asked, "How are we going?" as she could see no vehicle for them, and she was shocked and horrified when told they were to travel per dray on top of the luggage, furniture, etc. They landed at Peach Tree Experimental Farm six weeks later, which is now called Bukali.*
>
> *Provision for the trip had to be taken with them. When the bread was all used up the men made dampers in the ashes. Granny said she could not eat that dirty bread cooked in the dirt so she filled David's pockets with "taties" (potatoes) and that was her bread.*
>
> *One day she said she would go and get water and boil the billies. She came back and said, "There is no water down there, only what the Dirty Claughty Beasties is drinking". You need to hear this story related by a Scotsman to get the effect!*

Landholders held huge areas of land which was divided into smaller areas and settlements, and towns formed later. Monto was the largest town. These holdings were very large and very sparsely populated — the nearest neighbour miles away. Baileys family were at Old Cannindah, Cania Station at Moonford, Mulgildie Homestead not far from Monto.

Granny said the "pickerninnies" used to sneak and peep in the windows — they were very amused to see curtains at windows and coverings on the floor.

Herb Bailey was around Jack's age and used to tell us very funny incidents. One day the kids came across a dingo. After a little argument Herbie said, "It's a dingo". Jack said, "My father telt me it's a dingo and he kens". (In our language that means "he knows"). From Peach Tree Experimental Station (later named Bukali), the family moved to Monal.

When they were living at Monal provisions were purchased in Gladstone (100 miles away), and the teams collected them every three or four months — sacks of flour, bags of sugar and potatoes, and onions, etc. to last till the next trip. One trip Dad used to tell us about was when one wagon was overturned going up the range, called "Gentle Annie", provisions were strewn everywhere. The children had Christmas by stuffing themselves with all the goodies they could salvage. The children thought it was fun and wished it happened more often. When this type of accident happened the men unhooked the horses from the back team and hooked them on to the front horses which made a 24-horse team.

Geographical Map of the Area Surrounding Monto

This district is now known as the Upper Burnett.

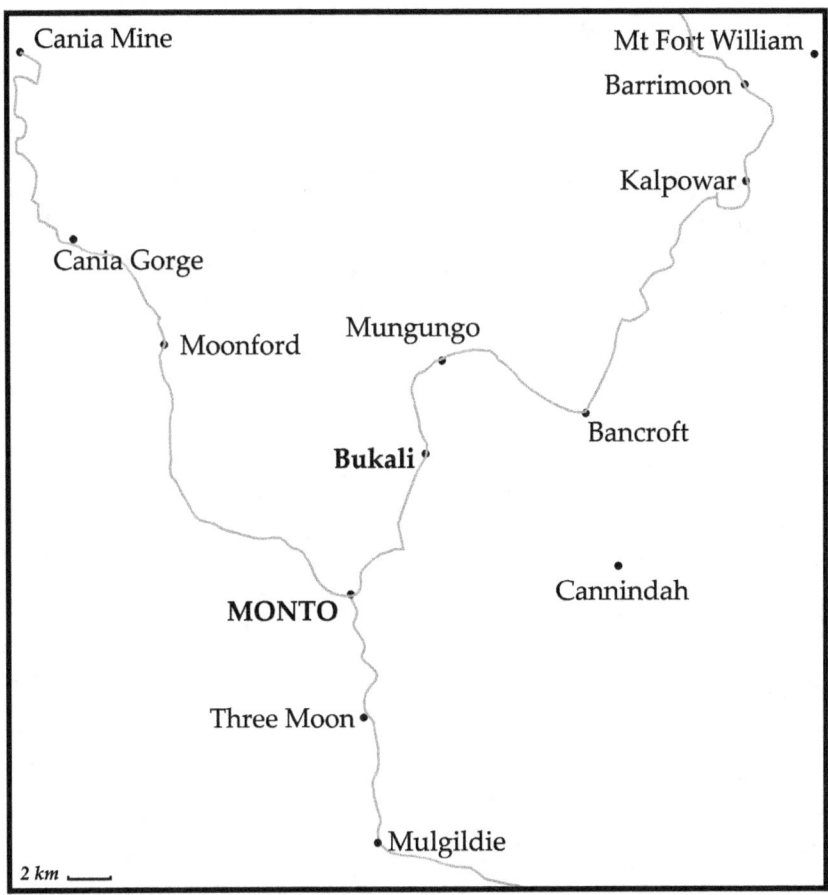

MY CONTEXT

I have written this book based on my memories as a child growing up in the Upper Burnett, as well as researching the internet to fill in gaps in the history of these relatives. While, these pioneering years are before my time, they nevertheless are included to give context as to how my forebears came to be in Australia. The next chapter, *The Early Years* are also before my time but give the direct back-story and context to what was my life in the bush in my formative years. It has occurred to me some folk today would ask, "Why did these people go to these God-forsaken places?" Keep reading and your questions will be answered!

INTRODUCTION TO THE EARLY DAYS

1855
Queensland was Part of a Big Wide Country

Thanks to Margaret List (Myles) for the research into the background and the history of these properties, as well as bringing to light the names of old pioneering families who have integrated into the Upper Burnett, and made it their forever home. Some of these family names are familiar to me.

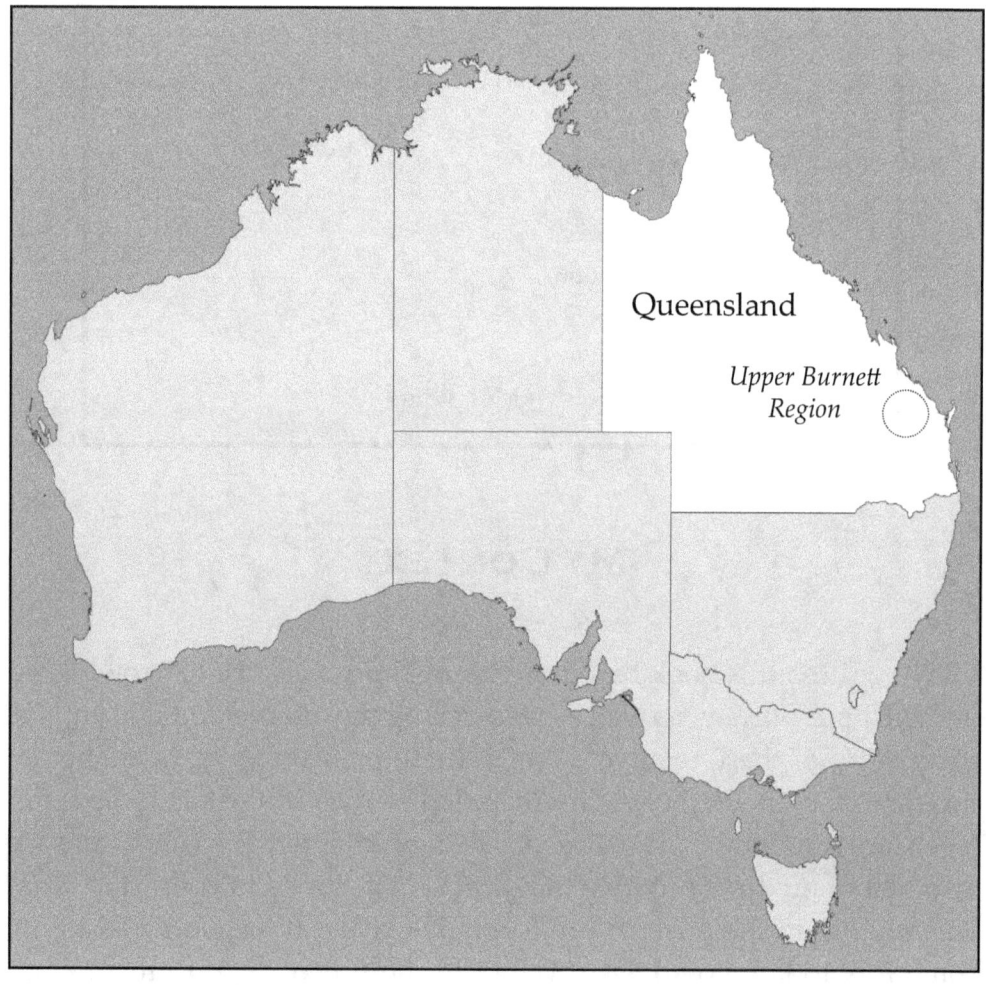

1855–1897
CANIA STATION/CLONMEL/YARROL

Extracted, credit to Helen Aitken and Maud Hampson:

On 24th July 1876 Cania was sold to McCord and Knox from Eidsvold Station for 30,876 pounds. There is a familiar name "McCord" who also was named as sponsoring my mother's grandfather David Myles (Snr) from Scotland to work at the Experimental Station at Bukali.

The only connection people had to the outside world when Aitken was manager was by Coach mail from Mt Perry (Angus Russell) and Eidsvold (Peter Bannah). Twice a year a wagon load of supplies came from Eidsvold. A train load of bullocks started off from the Station for a three-week trip to the train head, first at Ideraway and later Gayndah. 1897 mobs were sent to Swifts at Gladstone at an approximate droving cost of 8c per head. Interestingly, it is quoted that 500 to 600 weaners (young beasts) needed 6 to 8 drovers to do the job.

Also mentioned:

Mr Myles, a farmer from Scotland, grew lucerne on Monal Creek, cutting the lucerne with a scythe and baled it with an old hay press and distributed it by bullock wagon.

1914–1920
WORLD WAR I

Credit to Google:

World War I was a major negative shock for the Australian economy. Between 1914 and 1920 real aggregate gross domestic product declined by almost 10 percent. In stark contrast to World War II, when the economy grew strongly.

1916–1976
GOLDEN PLATEAU, CRACOW, QLD

I was born at Cracow in 1938, and at this time there was a Gold Rush.

Credit to the National Library of Australia:

> *Gold was first discovered in Cracow in 1875 by itinerant fossickers and a further discovery of a nugget was made by an Aboriginal stockman, Johnny Nipps in 1916. In 1931, the Golden Plateau mine was established and it operated continuously until 1976.*
>
> *Cracow State School opened on 12 June 1933. It was moved in 1935 after a young boy drowned in a nearby creek. The school remained there until its closure on 12 December 1997. The school building was moved to a nearby cattle station, Cracow Station.*

Cracow Station

> *Cracow Station is one of the oldest properties in the Dawson Callide region, having been settled in 1851 by John Mackenzie-Ross. He named Cracow after the Polish city of Krakow which he admired for its crucial role in Polish independence movements. Over the ensuing 50 years, Cracow became established sheep and cattle run. The seasons and market conditions weren't always kind, however, and it changed hands several times during that period. By far the greatest devastation occurred in 1902 at the crux of the infamous Federation drought when all except 36 of the station's 5000-odd head of cattle perished leaving the owner financially bereft and the station for sale once again.*

Two Roads into Cracow

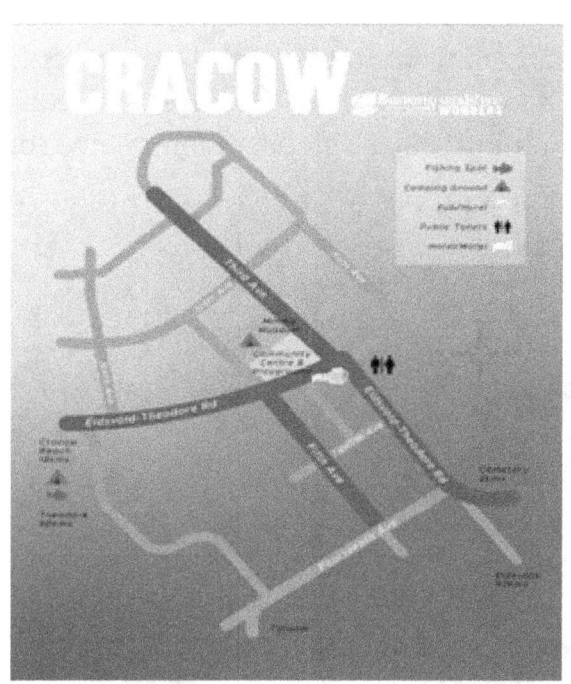

One road goes via Eidsvold, the other via Theodore in the Dawson Valley.

During a recent school reunion at Theodore, I took this opportunity to drive 50km to Cracow to refresh my childhood memories. While visiting the Cracow Museum, I took some photos of pictures hanging on the wall.

Cracow Post Office opened on 1 October 1932 and was destroyed in a fire in 2006. At its gold mining peak, the town included five cafes, barber shop, billiard saloon, two butchers, a picture theatre and a soft drink factory. The closure of the mine led to Cracow becoming a ghost town with many deserted houses and shops. In 2004, Newcrest Mining re-established gold mining in the town, leading to hopes the town may recover. This mine is now operated by Aeris Resources. The shops are vacant although the hotel remains open.

The Cracow Hospital

My parents, Rose and Steve Hansen, went to live with Dad's parents Bertha & Harry Hansen at Cracow and stayed a couple of years; fortunately, the hospital was built in 1930 and in operation in time for my birth.

The hospital under construction at Cracow
Source: Betty Lockley

People on the Move

There were a lot of men out of work, they had left their families, packed their "swag", grabbed a sugar bag and carried a lump of corn meat and loaf of bread and headed north, south, east or west riding their push bike looking for work and odd jobs. Hence the name "swagman" came about.

My grandfather David Charles Myles (Jnr) was extremely good at handling horse teams as you will see as more chapters show photos of the type of jobs he undertook either when carrying goods from settlement to settlement, and as well as working in the mines. With the lack of money, the lack of facilities and roads, bullock and horse teams were common place.

1900
CANIA MINE

Reported by Qld Places:

The Cania mining field was worked intermittently, with river dredging in about 1900. Most of the grazing land was under pastoral leases running until 1918.

Credit to Wikipedia:

Prior to the gold rushes in Australia, in the mid-19th century, bullock drays carried essential food and station supplies to isolated country areas. On return trips they transported wheat, wool, sugar cane and timber by drays drawn by teams of draught animals (either bullocks or horses) to shipping ports before the advent of rail. They travelled constantly across the landscape, servicing the pastoral stations and settlements far from regional transport hubs and urban centres. Some of the larger stations maintained their own teams for local use when harvesting and transporting wool. Both bullock and horse wagons carried heavy loads of wool and wheat which was the main produce transported over long distances, plus chaff and hay. A bullock wagon could only travel approximately three miles an hour (depending on the load and terrain) therefore it was slower than a horse team).

1900
BULLOCK TEAMS REPLACING HORSE TEAMS

Credit Department of Mines, report for 1933:

Bullock and horse teams were used to carry heavy loads on the way to the Monal goldfields.

During the early years the bullock tracks were very rough with narrow, steep "pinches", plus dangerous river and creek crossings. Many roads still follow the tracks made by bullock teams as they negotiated their way up or down hills via a winding course to make haulage easier.

Credit to Gleneden Farm for their explanation:

Bullock teams were renowned for their steady, patient and determined pull in difficult situations where horses were prone to jerkiness and panic leading to expensive injuries and breakages. Bullocks didn't often need shoeing and could live and work on rough herbage rather than the expensive feed required by working horses. It wasn't until improved road surfaces meant that the greater strength and speed of draught horses could be put to advantage that bullock teams began to be displaced on the road.

A bullock team at Cania

No changes to the life style happened in a hurry, and in the main, it would take about ten years for the transition to take place. The reasons were the lack of money to buy stock, harness/chains, finding/designing the right tools to do the job, having a means to get the things produced on site.

By the time I was born the emphasis had gone from bullock drawn wagons to horse drawn ploughs, drays and sulkies.

1880–1919
Christian Andersen
Blacksmith

Extracted from Queensland Bell Makers:

Christy Andersen established a large blacksmith shop in Miles and with the help of numerous assistants he made many 'Condamine' and 'Kentucky' bells from about 1880 to 1919. After that, he and his son Fred, continued bell production in Brisbane.

Christy's work was invaluable as he made tools, and invented methods to assist the mine workers before venturing west.

Christy (C.C.S. Andersen)

Fortunately, Christy — having been my dad's grandfather — had taught him a lot of skills. Christy made Condamine Bells and Kentucky Bells at his Smithy shop, and it is now available to the public at the Miles Museum, Queensland.

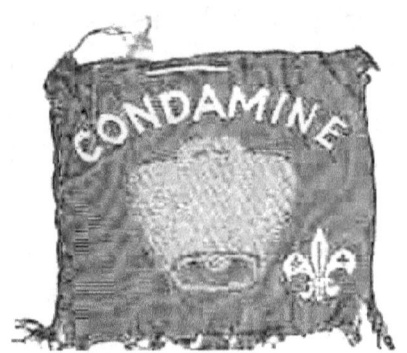

Geographical Map of the Toowomba, Dalby, Miles area

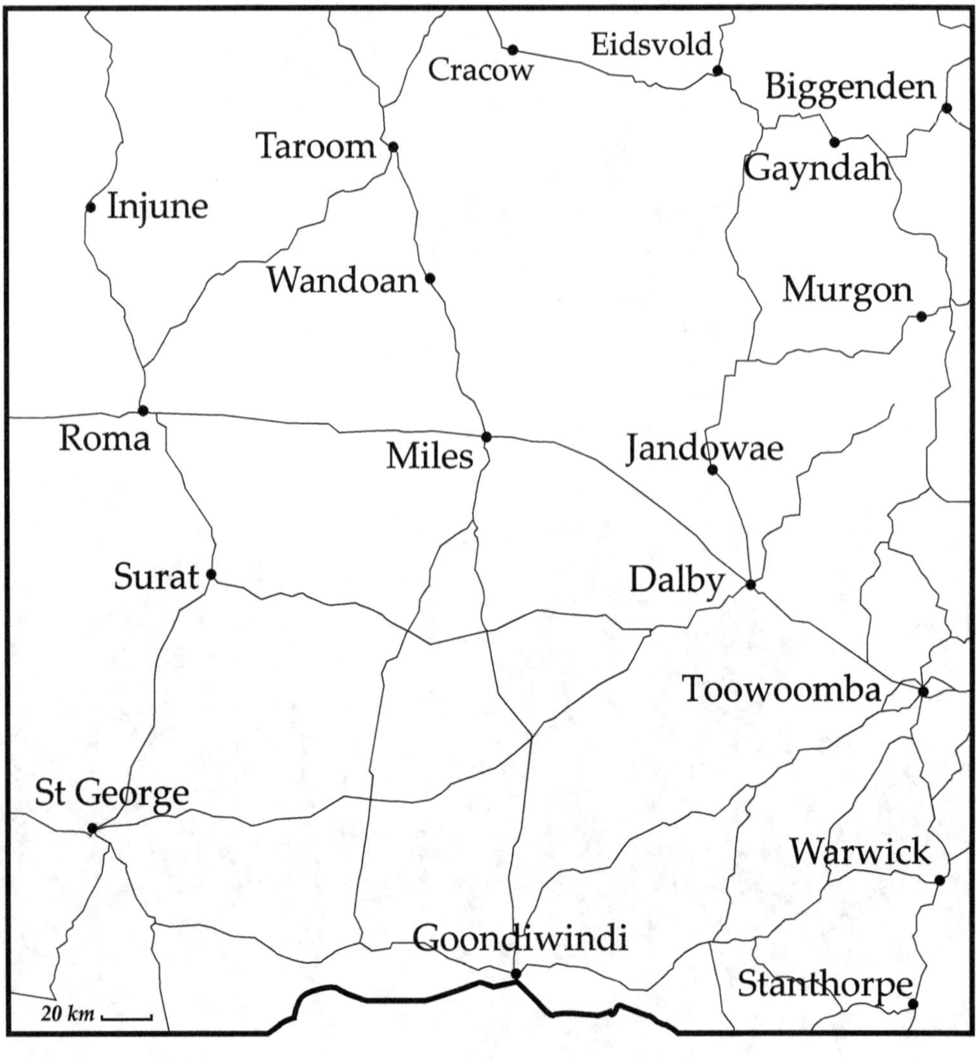

1891–1912
Monal Mine

Courtesy of Monto Magic:

The first gold was found in Monal in 1891 and the official gold field was proclaimed 1892. Mining for gold ceased in about 1912 but resumed on a small scale in the mid 1930's.

At one stage the town of Monal supported three hotels: Cosmopolitan, Royal & The Bush Rat, *as well as two butcher shops and general stores and were looked after by George Williams & Arthur Clewley. Stores & mail came from Gladstone by coach up the steep Dawes Range at a place known as Gentle Annie. When going down the range a large tree would be felled and attached to the back axle to steady things down. When traveling up the Monal Creek, the first sign of the old township is the cemetery on the right. There are two fenced graves and many unmarked graves. In 2000 a set of wagon wheels and a plaque with the known names, ages & occupations of the people that were laid to rest at Monal was unveiled as a permanent reminder of what people gave to make a living in the pioneering days.*

Horse teams at Monal

Geographical Maps of Upper Burnett & Boyne Valley Mining towns

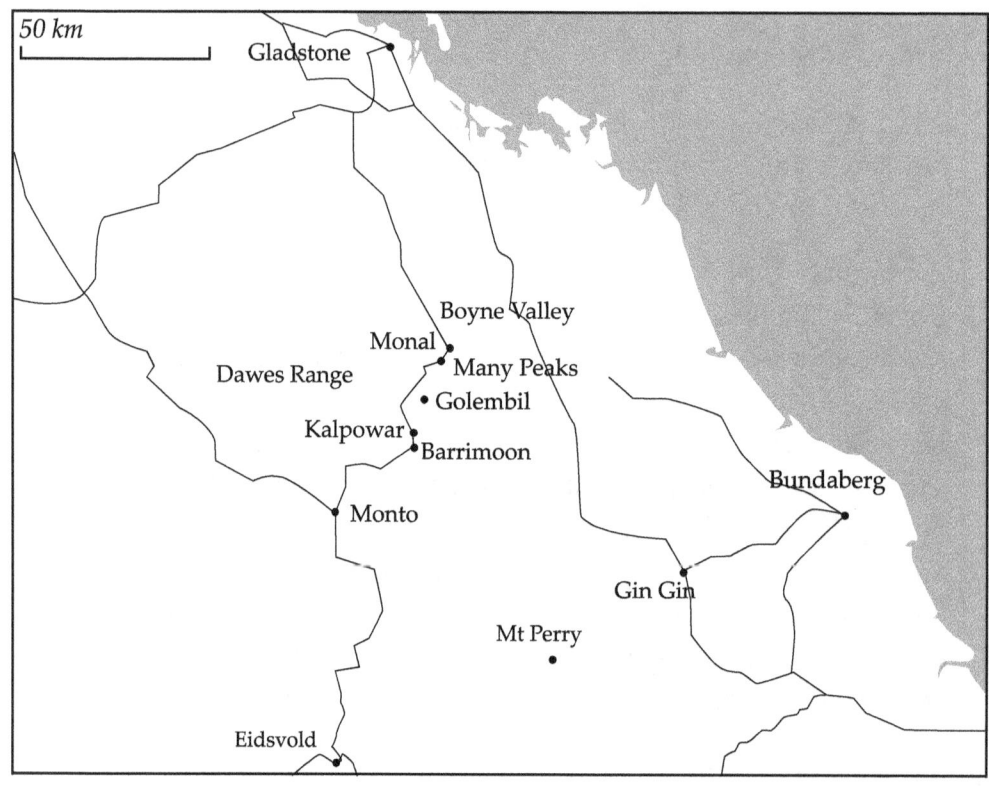

1890
Monal Mine

Stompers

Courtesy of Monto Magic:

These stompers were used to crush up the stones.

Steam Boiler

Credit Monto Magic:

The first Steam Boiler was brought by horse team from Mt Perry by George Blundell, in about the mid 1890s.

At Monal a boiler had got bogged as it veered off the dirt road. This picture shows my grandfather David Myles Jnr, with his hand on hip contemplating what to do.

Note the hurricane lantern on the ground at the lefthand corner of the picture; probably to show others going down the road there was a hazard. The photo shows the boiler had been put back upright, propped up, and a rope was attached to a tree to keep it from falling over into the ditch.

Cornish Boiler

It took several horse teams to pull this huge boiler over Gentle Annie (a very steep slope). I saw the boiler; it was as big as a train engine. Dave Myles Jnr my grandfather had his horse team involved with this mine project.

The big Cornish boiler was brought from Gladstone a few years later, up the Dawes Range. A team of 62 horses were used to bring it up the range; the pick of 5 teams and five drivers, including Marshall Goody, Davey Myles, Tom Flynn & Max Williams.

Glassford Creek Chimneys

Credit to Helen Goody for her photo of the Glasford Creek chimneys from the copper smelter.

Credit to Monto Magic:

> *Glassford was a gold & copper mining township during the late 1800s & early 1900s located on Little Glassford Creek (also known as Coppermine Creek). There were originally two townships in the area. One at the mine & another about 4km downstream. The top township is where the chimneys and old mining equipment are located. There is little to no evidence of anything of the downstream township.*

1910
MONAL TOWNSHIP

Courtesy of Monto Magic:

The Monal Town Reserve was established in 1910.

Three of my uncles were born at Monal: Charley, 1905; Jim, 1907; Alfred, 1908.

Monal Goldfields School

1903
Mary Russell Teaching Appointment

MARY'S TEACHING APPOINTMENT

Reference Numbers: 8394 R.
To be quoted in your reply: 8222·03

DEPARTMENT OF PUBLIC INSTRUCTION,

Brisbane, 4th June, 1903.

MEMORANDUM TO Miss Mary Russell,
Provisional School,
Monal.

Through the Head Teacher.

In compliance with the request contained in your letter of the 26th ultimo, I have to intimate that the Minister has been pleased to approve of your appointment to the position of Head Teacher of the Provisional School at Monal from the 1st July, proximo.

Your emoluments will be salary at the rate of £90 per annum, subject to adjustment in accordance with Clause 66 of the Regulations.

A. G. Anderson
Under Secretary.

1904
David Myles (Jnr) and Mary Russell Wed

Mary Russell aged 19, married David Charles Myles (Jnr), aged 22. They lived at Monal, and then moved to Many Peaks with their three children. The fourth Catherine (Cass) was born at Gladstone 1910; seven more babies were born at Many Peaks.

We affectionately called David Myles (Jnr) 'Pa' and his wife Mary Russell was 'Ma'.

Frances Myles (Punch) Shanty at Monal

Frances (Punch) Myles and Myrtle had seven children: William, Alan, Shirley, Kenny, Mervyn, Vera, and Eric.

1916
David Myles (Snr) — Grave Site

Grave of David Myles (Snr) following our family reunion.

2006

At a family reunion some local relatives agreed to upgrade the picket fence and make good David Myles'(Snr) grave. Without maintenance the history of Monal will slowly disappear.

Thanks to Billy Myles (RIP), Joan Derrick (Myles) and Andrew Myles for their help. Copperfield Creek runs at the base of the Monal mine site.

2022

Ann and Geoff Ludlow fossicking for gold!

Margaret List (Myles) standing. Rita Paulos (Hansen) sitting.

1845–1924
MANY PEAKS

Geographical Map of the Boyne Valley

The map below will give a perspective to the distance between Many Peaks, Gladstone and Mt Perry, as well as the expansive area the workers could travel to get work.

Courtesy of Queensland Places:

> The Many Peaks mine was worked continuously until 1918, and during its life Many Peaks' population peaked at 1300. When mining ended in the mid-1920s, sawmilling, local dairying and grazing continued, but population rapidly declined. By 1924 all that remained of the Many Peaks township was a hotel and a row of houses. The hotel provides a welcome highway stop, while the hospital has been transferred to neighbouring Builyan. Within a few years Many Peaks had a progress association, a hospital (1910), a courthouse, Anglican and Catholic churches, up to five hotels and a silent picture show. Pugh's Directory (1924) also recorded five drapers, an aerated waters manufacturer and a sawmill.

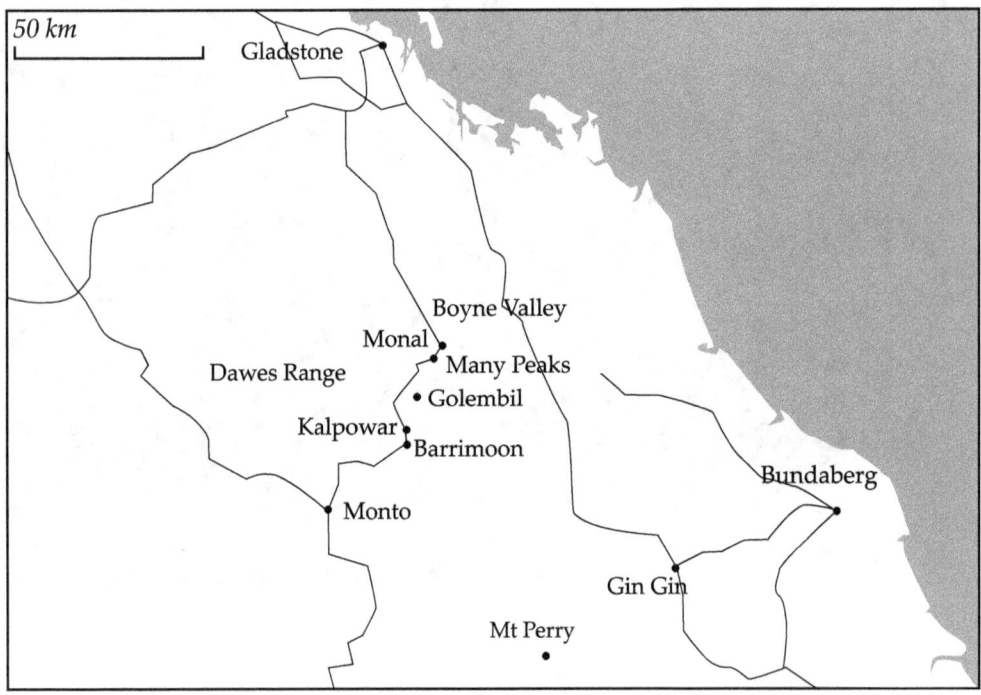

1898–1910
MANY PEAKS COPPER MINE

Courtesy of Qld Places:

The Many Peaks copper find occurred in 1896, and a Mount Morgan syndicate acquired the mining rights in 1898. In 1906 it was decided that the ore would be most profitably processed if transported to Mount Morgan for use as a flux in the smelters there. A railway line was built in 1910, incidentally opening up much of the Boyne Valley's timber and dairy produce to vastly improved transportation.

The mine workings

1920
Many Peaks Township

These photos had been passed down through the family, and have handwriting on the bottom identifying each photo. This is the main street of Many Peaks.

Morgan Street looking west

Note the walk bridge over the creek, on the left, then a walk up the hill to the Myles family home.

Imperial Hotel

Note a large horse team setting out from Many Peaks for Mt Cannindah.

Main Street, Many Peaks

1907
Epidemics

Diphtheria

Credit to The Chronicle, March 30, 1907:

> *The Burial Ground in Moy Pocket Road Gheerulla was established by the community in 1907 to provide a resting place for two little girls, Florrie May and Ivy Christiana Hansen who died of diphtheria before medical assistance could reach them from Nambour.*

This article refers to my dad's two eldest sisters who contracted diphtheria in 1907 and passed away one day apart aged 4 and 7 years. They are laid to rest at the Gheerulla Cemetery near Kenilworth, Sunshine Coast district.

There was always the fear of diphtheria, tetanus, scarlet fever, whooping cough and polio since vaccinations were not available. We did not learn to swim as kids and were not allowed to go swimming in any dirty creeks because of the risk of infection from these deadly diseases, especially diphtheria.

Scarlet Fever

The names listed on the plaque shows of lives lost at Monal and buried in the cemetery. Sadly, this plaque has the names of 13 young children who had passed away, buried at the Monal Mine Cemetery.

1920
VACCINATIONS

Immunisation

Following on my previous chapter regarding the epidemics of the past and the devastating loss of young children, diphtheria and polio vaccines were finally available.

Information from Google:

> *1920 — Diphtheria toxoid was developed in the early 1920s but was not widely used until the early 1930s. It was incorporated with tetanus toxoid and pertussis vaccine and became routinely used in the 1940s.*

> *Polio — In 1955, Salk developed the inactivated poliovirus vaccine; thus, began widespread immunisation. This was followed in 1960 by a live, attenuated oral vaccine developed by Sabin. The effect was impressive. From 28,000 reported cases of polio in 1955, in 1956, one year after immunisation, there were only 15,000 cases.*

1920–30s
BOYNE VALLEY RAILWAY TUNNELS

Golembil to Barrimoon

The section from Monto down into the Boyne Valley was the last section built in the 1920 and 30s. Incidentally the first section of this railway line was commenced in 1910 to transport copper and ore from Many Peaks to Mt Morgan.

Our grandfather David Myles (Junior) used his bullock and horse teams while working on this project that took more than ten years to complete.

This train line took me to Gladstone on part of my journey to boarding school in 1952/53. Locals who lived on the Monto to Gladstone line relied on the train services for hospital and medical appointments in Gladstone.

As part of our cousin trip in 2022 we visited the tunnels which are now used as a rail trail for walkers, horse and bicycle riders between Golembil and Barrimoon.

1914–1920
Horse and Wagon Transport

1920 Chas Gassman's horse teams

Hauling produce

Ferny Hills, Brisbane

Uncle Jack Myles (Pa's brother) hauling logs.

1923
Dooboon

Story courtesy of Genealogy:

Dooboon was the Aboriginal name for the ironbark trees in the area. John (Jack) Stapleton selected Dooboon when the mining started on his property. He started a hotel in the area. In 1923 John Stapleton sold Dooboon to Eric Ball. Who sold it to Ray Drinkwater in 1996. Before taking up Dooboon, John Stapleton was well known around the Burnett and Kolan districts, having opened the first hotels to be built at Gin Gin and Wallaville. The hotel at Wallaville was called the Bluebell because of the large bell-shaped construction on the roof in the shape of a bell, and which was painted blue. Being a gold field meant there were many brawls and fights in the pub. The prospectors would come in of a weekend to weight their gold, and drink and brawl for the weekend.

Dooboon Hotel

This is my grandfather David Myles (Jnr) with his horse team outside the Dooboon Hotel.

1924–2022
Monto

Google reports:

The township of Monto came into existence in 1924 as a consequence of the Land Development Scheme. A few very large properties were resumed to provide prime agricultural land for returning soldiers and pioneer settlers.

1924 Newton Street

1926 Newton Street

2022 Newton Street

2022 Post Office/Exchange

2022 Monto Shire Council

2022 Grand Hotel

2022 Albert Hotel

2022 New Royal Hotel

2022 Water Tower Monto

Grain Silos Monto

These silos are a spectacle seen as driving south out of Monto.

1927
BUILDING THE SILVERWOOD DAM
Renamed The Connolly Dam

Academic Accelerator reports:

The Connolly Dam, also known as the Silverwood Dam, is a rockfill levee dam with gateless spillway crossing Rosenthal Creek and Fitz Creek and is located in the area of Silverwood in the South Downs region, part of the Darling Downs District. The dam's primary purpose is to provide drinking water to the Southern Downs region. It flows through the Rosenthal River and joins the Condamine River east of Warwick.

My Dad worked on this project as a young man.

Lodgings for Workers

You can see pipes leading from the roof of the shack into the small tank at the back of the hut; face and hand washing would be done from the tap of the tank using the tank stand as a bench for the basin and bar of soap.

My Dad (Tib Hansen) was 14 years old; he appears to be having lunch with tools at his feet, and his push bike lying on the ground. I noticed rope threaded through the spokes of Dad's pushbike to replace tyres.

1926–1969
The Transition Years

Grandpa's and Grandma's Place

This photo of Mary Russell, and David Myles (Jnr) was taken at Margaret Myles (granddaughter's wedding in 1963).

In 1926 my Mum's whole family moved from Many Peaks to Branch Creek in the Bancroft district. Pa continued with his horse team carting provisions to the residents in the Gladstone, Dooboon (Mt Perry) and Upper Burnett districts.

Branch Creek — The Homestead

Mum's two older brothers Jim and Charley horsing around in front of the homestead. See Ma looking over the railing in the background.

From my early memory the homestead was a huge sprawling house resembling two buildings joined in the middle with a covered way type of entry, with lots of steps. The kitchen and dining room, with a huge table and stools that would seat about 20/30 people, combustion stove, huge pantry, adjoined by a boys' dormitory, and a small verandah that housed a big parrot cage, formed the addition as shown on the left in this picture. The area to the right lead into the girl's rooms, parents retreat, and large lounge with a piano, and was surrounded by a verandah on three sides. It was home to 11 siblings. The family built a tennis court that got a lot of use while the family was growing up. The mode of transport was by horseback.

This property was isolated, situated about 30 miles from the Mungungo pub, and 4 neighbours were about 3 to 8 miles away. As time went by the older boys acquired properties within the district and would often be calling in and assisting with the mustering and dipping.

1941

*Rita (me) pedalling my three-wheeler horse,
nursing cousin Barry Myles on Dargen*

This photo was taken at Branch Creek; see the stumps for the homestead on the right. On the left there is a fenced off area which was where a special cool room was built, about 6m x 6m, high pitched roof, with a cement floor and 1m high cement sides, and flywire covering the upper sides. All large perishable items would be stored, e.g. cream cans, meat, to keep them cool and safe from hot weather, flies, stray animals, and so on.

2006

This is the homestead as it stands, 80 years on. In about 1946 the boy's dormitory that had been added on the left of the house was demolished and timber used to build a holiday shack at Tannum.

Learning by Correspondence

Grandma was a school teacher in her early life and she was busy passing on some mathematical skills and literacy skills to the children. Everybody in the house had to "pull their weight"; the girls would say the boys did not pull their weight and were allowed to go 'roo shooting to get pocket money while the three youngest girls were working in the dairy! The two older boys preferred to go out with their dad handling horses rather than settle down to learn school work.

Pa's Morning routine

I speak about the 1940's. Each morning Pa's jobs were to light the combustion stove, and boil the kettles, ready for breakfast. His favourite breakfast was toast made with a very large fork held over the hot coals, eaten with a big slice of cheese, and a cup of tea. Always a 5lb block of mature cheese, wrapped in cheesecloth, would be on the kitchen table. Pa would devour the chunky slices on toast.

Music was a part of having a social life

The piano remained in the lounge room until Ma and Pa passed away. The lounge room was the hub of any gathering of the family, and kids had to behave and make little noise if they wanted to stay in this huge adult lounge room.

The older siblings, Alf, Cass, and Claudia had the opportunity to learn piano.

I must add that my Uncle Alf passed away at 99.5 years old and was still playing bowls, playing the piano and driving his car for miles; my Aunt Cass passed away at 98 years old and continued playing the piano until she had a stroke a couple of years earlier. My theory is that music brings a lot of harmony into people's lives; plus, hard work does not kill people.

Whip cracking

Under the house at the homestead was a kid's minefield and there was always something to do, and things to explore. The wooden posts had pegs bored into the side to hang the horse harness, e.g. saddles, bridles, saddlebags, saddlecloths, whips, etc, to get them off the ground. The whips were like toys for me to play with, and many a day I wrapped a whip around my legs or neck trying to swing it around. To crack a whip was quite an achievement for a kid.

Horse and Sulky

Once a year my Mum would be taken to town for a dental check, and with her going to town outfit on, she would pile into the horse drawn sulky for the ride to Monto. It would take a whole day to get to and from town, probably only travelling about 5 and 10 miles per hour.

Photo credit to eHive collection of 1930.

It was years before a car got parked underneath the house. As Pa could not drive, plus cars were not invented until he was in his 50s, he would transport the family by horse and sulky.

Until the early 1940s various breeds of horses had a big part to play in people's lives, i.e. saddle horses, draft horses, race horses, and ponies were the main mode of transport.

Horse and Dray

Hay, wood, water and grain was transported by horse and dray, ploughing was by single furrow plough pulled by a draught horse.

State Library of South Australia PRG 280/1/15/70

Double Bank — Quiet Horses for Children

My Aunt Cass would take me double-bank to see her parents (Ma and Pa) and we would take short-cuts through the bush tracks, and follow the dividing fences to the wire gates to gain entry to the next property.

1930 Social Life at Branch Creek

Social life would often be combined with working life. When jobs were needed to be done a thermos of tea, and a snack would be packed up to make it an enjoyable time, and at the same time achieving a goal, e.g. fixing a fence, replacing a fence post, carting wood for the stove.

There was no power, although in time some lucky farmers had generators, mostly to run the milking machines. There were always jobs to be done, like milking the cows twice daily, plus mustering, feeding the pigs and poddies and planting crops. Gradually, Branch Creek dedicated an area of ground to grow fruit trees; a fenced off area down by the creek. There was an orchard feeling when entering the area as the variety of trees ranged from mulberry, oranges, lemons, figs and persimmons.

Tennis

With a family of eleven siblings, there was enough for a couple of tennis teams. Ant bed tennis courts were popular, and required watering and rolling to keep the surface in good condition. Without power or sewerage connected, water was collected in tanks connected to the house, or carted from the well.

Two of the older siblings played instruments which was a great asset when planning a social calendar.

Saturday Night Dances

The older siblings would ride their horses to dances about 10 miles away. Instruments like piano accordion, violin, cornet, saxophone and mouth organ would be carried in a sugar bag swung over the rider's shoulder.

The Younger Siblings at Branch Creek

Enjoying time with the farm animals

This photo was taken in 1935; left to right, Doll, Rose, Ene on the horse with her brother Roland, and Valroy on the white horse; they are the children of Dave and Mary Myles.

Swimming Holes

The favourite swimming spot would be used in the summer time. The water had to be clear, indicating the water was fresh, and running in one end and out the other to prevent stale water breeding bacteria.

Shooting Season

After the war there was a bounty paid by the authorities for the fox and dingo scalps. Shooting seasons were put in place allowing a culling out of nuisance animals. This provided a bit extra pocket money for the farmer/stockman who were handy with a gun.

There was also duck season, introduced as wild ducks were a delicacy when money was so scarce. Dad would take advantage of these times especially for Christmas and Easter times. Luckily, he was a good shot as it was important to aim for the head, leaving the rest of the body untouched. The dog was trained to fetch the duck out of the water.

Margaret List (Myles) Memories of Branch Creek

Introducing another cousin, Margaret, who has kindly shared her many memories of life at Branch Creek with Ma and Pa:

My first memory of Branch Creek was being driven to the Doctor in Monto to have stitches in my head.

During the drought times in 1945 cattle food was scarce. When an animal became weak it was given help to stand, either in a sling or was given extra in the form of hay to eat. I was obviously milking the cow when Dad was mustering his horses to go on a droving trip taking animals to the Meat Works in Gladstone. On this occasion one of the horses jumped the rails and proceeded to help itself to the cow's food. I must have chased the horse and consequently it kicked me in the head. Living in the country with no phone or motor vehicle, Dad took me on horseback to the grandparents' home (Branch Creek) some miles away. I remember Uncle Alf and Dad (Jim) driving me to Monto in the dark and the Doctor stitching my head, and spending days in the Monto Hospital. As a consequence, I seemed to spend a lot of time as a young child at my grandparents' home. I think that was really an opportunity for Grandma to start my schooling but I don't remember doing any lessons. However, Grandpa was still dairying at that time. We would get up early and Pa teaching me to make toast with a toasting fork on the stove and the slices of thick cheese we had before heading off to round up the cows before milking. Pa

also taught me how to ride a horse so these mornings were special helping with the milking, running the cream separator and feeding the poddies. We went home to a cooked breakfast! My connection to my Grandparents went into my teenage years and beyond.

When WW2 ended is about the time Ma and Pa were thinking about their retirement, and their son Alf was a returned soldier, encouraged them to look at Tannum Sands for a piece of land. They managed to acquire land in a ballot, 647sqm block of land looking over the ocean. This land came with conditions that stated only 50 pounds worth of improvements could be done yearly. Since building materials were scarce it was decided to demolish the section that housed the boy's dormitory (the part of Branch Creek to the left of the front steps) and cart it to Tannum. It was a DIY project that my Uncle Arthur Hansen took on, spending many weekends constructing a seaside dwelling. Just of a matter of interest this property in Coral Street was sold in December 2009 for 720,500 dollars.

2022

Here are 3 of Ma and Pa's grandchildren — Dawn Ludlow, Rita Paulos and Carol Gassman — having lunch at Tannum with a view, just 200m from the Coral Street property.

Margaret List (Myles) Research

Here is a brief summary of Margaret's trip to Ireland in 2017 chasing records of our grandparents:

My connection to my grandparents went into my teenage years and beyond. We were aware that both grandparents came from overseas in their early years from Scotland, and Grandma Mary Margaret nee Russell was born in Northern Ireland at Armah where her parents lived in the county of Corlust. She was the eldest child of 11 children. Her father was John Russell of Glascow and her mother was Isabella Muldrew. John Russell joined the Royal Army Medical Corps (as recorded in the British Army WW1 Service Records 1914/1920) when Mary was a baby. They moved to Australia in 1888/89. John died in 1916 and Isabella many years later. They are both buried in the Cemetery in Ipswich.

On the last day of my visit to Ireland, Donald drove to Markethall and we met John and his wife in the Butcher shop. John was unable to give many details of the family and, unfortunately, his father who was into family history was away on holidays. John told us the family had previously done up a family history called Fallen Blossoms *but he did not have a copy. I understood that as far as he was aware most of the Muldrew family had gone to America, a few to France; he also said there were some connections to the Japanese. John directed us to his cousin who owned the Pub across the road whose mother was a Muldrew. We met her, Nan Rice. We visited her parent's graves in the Cremorne Cemetery later in the day. Ireland is a beautiful place. Then, as Donald drove us into the country with narrow bitumen one lane roads noticing dairy farms and fodder crops everywhere. Donald who lived all his life in Ireland was of Catholic decent remarked, "We are in Protestant country," and that was mind boggling. We sought help from any community and farms along the way seeking to find Corlust. With Corlust written on a cream can at the entry to the property we went in and, unfortunately, the lady a school teacher, could not give us any history of Corlust Country. She said the land was purchased about 10 years ago and the house built on it.*

We were warned to take extra care on the narrow roads as the Milk Tankers were very active as were farmers moving machinery.

We did some research and found a lot of records of leases starting back as far as 1780, and found anomalies in the spelling of the name Muldrew, for example, spelt as McMuldrath, Muldragh or Mulldra.

Predators to Livestock

Dingoes

Google says:

> The dingo is an opportunistic and generalist predator that will search widely for food and eat whatever it finds. Dingoes generally eat small to medium native mammals.

Dingoes (often referred to as wild dogs) would often attack young calves, especially animals that were weak. This applied more to calves, sheep and goats being smaller animals.

Image: Rae Wallis

Image: Charles Jackson

Foxes

Foxes are very sly and sneaky animals, and they would dig under the fowl house enclosure for their prey. If the soil was soft or sandy it was often necessary to bury wire netting a foot into the ground to prevent them entering the chook pen by digging a hole under the fence.

Essential Farming Accessories

Wells and Windmills

Credit to Google:

> In 1871 George Griffiths set up a mechanical workshop in Toowoomba thus starting, what is now the Southern Cross Group of Engineering Companies. His first wooden framed windmills were built in 1876 and supplied to Jimbour Station at Dalby on the Darling Downs.

The paddocks had wells and windmills. The houses had high tank stands, for gravity feed, and every down pipe lead into a tank. Water was a precious commodity.

On properties out of town there is a need to be self-sufficient. For this reason, there were chooks (hens and roosters), milking cows, beef cattle, pigs, horses, draft-horses, stock whips, dips (for cattle tick control), and mustering. Vegetable patches were usually made at the top of the creek banks to allow easy access to water.

Gravity Fed Water Supplies

On rural properties, or those without town water supply, gravity feed was an economical way to have water laid on. The high tank stand would give enough pressure to carry water to lower buildings; and the only time a pump would be needed was to refill the elevated water tank.

Wire Gates in the Paddock

Property dividing fences have not changed much in all these years. They looked very much like this photo, and were usually made from two saplings forming the frame, or star pickets, and wire attached to the strainer post that formed a loop to insert the gate post, and pulled tight with a piece of sapling and slipped around making a sort of noose.

Grids made from local grown timber

The earlier grids made of saplings were bumpy.

Cattle Grids

The iron grid above was relatively smooth to cross.

Lavatory

The "dunny" (ablution house) at Branch Creek had two holes on the seat, one for big bums and one for smaller bums (the kids). Imagine the demand for a seat when there were 11 children in the family!

The spiders and flies were the main bother, though we always kept an eye out for a "Joe Blow" (snake). Usually when one left the "dunny" one's pants would be sprinkled with odd bits of saw dust (prickly stuff); old papers were in there too to be used as toilet paper, and of course for a little read!

These "dunnies" were an eyesore. If, or when septic or sewerage was connected, these small out buildings were handy. The disused lavatory made a great tool shed since they had been built on a cement base with a lockable door.

On the share farm we managed, the lavatory was built over a huge hole in the ground which saved the regular job of emptying the "dunny can".

Cattle Dipping

Cattle being held in a holding yard in preparation for their various procedures. The beast would be dipped by being pushed/jumping into a pesticide treated plunge dip, swim through, and then exit through the draining yard.

Dipping day was a special occasion, if I was allowed to be included. Most of the kids liked to take part, rounding up the cattle into the yards for dipping, and the "cutting-out" was exciting, separating the calves, weaners, and beef cattle. Separating the cattle was necessary so tasks like castration, branding, injections, etc. could be undertaken. Because bush reared stock does not like being handled, as they normally would roam around the paddocks without human contact. Dipping day often got the cattle stirred up. The crush leading into the dip was narrow which meant it was easier to restrain the beasts, and also for the safety of the handlers. The dogs were trained to help bring the cattle into the yards.

Cattle Dip

It was exciting as a kid to see a rescue at the dip. One bullock had rickets from zamia poisoning (noxious weed) and had trouble swimming through the dip, and it got half way, wanted to turn around (not possible), and got so tired it was going to drown, so it was all hands and yelling "Hoy, hoy" to urge this beast to keep treading water until it could reach the draining ramp/yard. Luckily this steer had huge horns so my Uncle George lassoed its horns, and was then able to lift the rope upwards, which helped lift the beasts head up, keeping the nostrils out  of the dip mixture. Those watching were yelling and banging the sides of the dip until finally this exhausted bullock was able to scramble into the dip-draining yard.

Branding

Branding is carried out in a crush, whether it is a home style or a professionally made crush. It must be strong as it has to withstand the weight of an animal just in case it should become enraged. When branding it is necessary to put the branding irons in a fire until the coals are red hot, and then plunge the metal shape (with registered numbers) onto the rump burning the hair, right to the skin, so it would not grow out. Branding is necessary as a method of identifying who owns the beast. If the beasts stray, cattle duffers steal, and at sale yards the brand is proof of ownership. Mostly the duffers would slaughter the cattle to destroy the evidence or just use them as breeders; in which case they would not make the sale yard in case the police were on their tracks.

Dip and Loading Ramp

After the dipping day was over some cattle might need to be transported to the sale yards, or segregated into paddocks. The truck would back up to the ramp, stock would be in the holding yard ready to head up the ramp onto the livestock trailer or truck.

Animal Love

Horse Breaking

Before a horse could be used for riding, there was some training to do with respect to having a saddle on its back; horses had to be trained to wear blinkers to stop them being startled if a loud object was coming into their space.

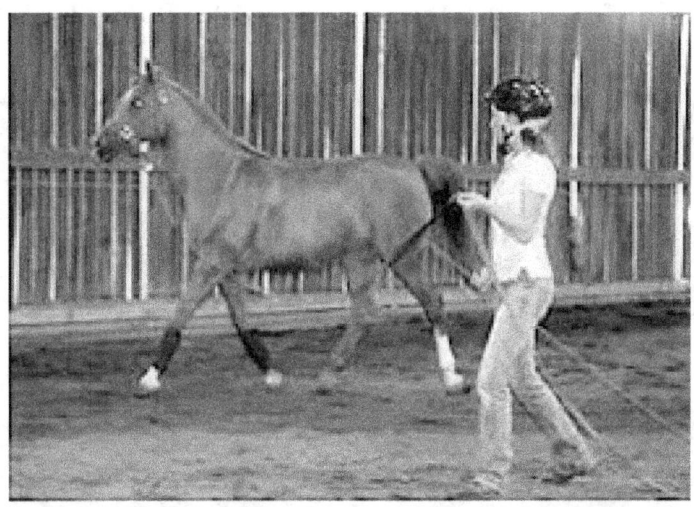

Another exciting day was when the horses would be tamed and prepared for riding (referred to as horse-breaking). The horse would be held in a stockyard, usually constructed of split timber poles. Stock yards had to be high, strong, and withstand a beast going ballistic once confined to a small space. I witnessed a horse breaking episode where about 3 days were spent handling this gelding to tame it; then yarded into a crush with a halter mounted over its head and a long rope attached. The gate would be opened into the pole pen and the handler would guide the horse around trying to get it to canter around in a circle. A tackling would be fitted over its body to get it used to the feel of a saddle. The bridle or halter would be attached to the tackling to keep the head down so it could not jump and rear, and if the horse was not co-operative blinkers would be fitted over the bridle so the beast had limited vision and not be so scared. The quieter the beast from the outset, having had human contact previously, the easier the job. The locally tamed horses and cows would not kick and carry-on and the kids could walk close without fear of being kicked. To tighten the girth (under the horse's tummy) was not something it liked, and when the gate was opened it would often buck furiously trying to get rid of the gear/tackling off its back. For any new comer to witness this type of horse handling was fascinating, and especially to kids.

It was the end of an era once Ma and Pa got too old to continue the lifestyle, we all enjoyed. Pa was always kind and would have a bottle of boiled lollies hidden away for us kids.

This chapter covers a lot of years, and really summarises what a life time in the country/bush/land consisted of. There was always something to do, and the rest was up to the initiative and motivation that person brought to the land.

The sad time came when the bachelor boys (Alf and George) stayed on the property and the final chapter was to sell Branch Creek, and it would then have new owners. Here is Uncle Alf trying to sort through the house goods and chattels to wind up the ownership.

The remains winding up the end of an era.

1920–1930s
Transition from Horse to Automobile

Google reports:

In the 1920s, horses were part of daily life across Australia. Over the following decade, however, the power and efficiency of the motor vehicle saw it rapidly replace harnessed horses for haulage and transport. By the 1930s, horses in urban areas had become a part of the past.

Travel

Local travel was mostly by horse, taking short-cuts through the horse tracks and neighbouring properties. The T-Model Ford was used to transfer the family from one campsite to another. Chains or ropes were carried and could be fitted over the car tyres to give the vehicle tyres traction in the wet weather, especially effective on a slippery muddy dirt road, or an incline up the creek bank. Creek crossings were usually wet since the crossings had lots of medium size stones with a few inches of water flowing downstream. It took years before these wet creek crossings were replaced with causeways (dry crossings made of concrete with a drainage pipe to take the flowing stream underneath).

Dicky Seat Passenger Car

Wikipedia reports:

A rumble seat, dicky seat, also called a mother-in-law seat, is an upholstered exterior seat which folded into the rear of a coach, carriage, or early motorcar. Depending on its configuration, it provided exposed seating for one or two passengers.

This model car did not take too many passengers unless one more passenger needed a seat and they would hitch a ride by hanging off the running-board the best way they could. Often, to make the vehicle more serviceable the back portion of the chassis was cut off and replaced with a wooden tray with a tail gate, and side seats for passengers.

My grandfather, Harry Hansen is on the right below in the white shirt. There is a canvas hood on this model motor car, and the door at the back could be opened to take an extra passenger.

I lived with my dad's parents (my grandparents) for a short time so I could attend school while Mum and Dad were assessing the possibilities of taking a few months off for 'roo shooting. Pop Hansen would drive me to school and I always liked going with him as he would "kangaroo" along. The older cars were manual and by using the handbrake, and then starting off by releasing the foot-brake, as well as engaging the accelerator and clutch on a bit of a slope, was not always smooth, hence the word "kangaroo" was my idea about the ride.

Ford Model T

In this photo my dad's two brothers' "Chook" and Don are looking at Pop Hansen's dicky seat car.

Our T Model had a canvas hood, and the utility tray at the back. In fact, my dad-built side seats off our Model T Ford's sides by fastening an L- shaped tray, enabling four extra passengers in the back. Often to get our Ford Model T started on a cold day it was necessary to use a crank handle to turn the pistons over, and then wait a while for the motor to warm up before take-off. If the motor was not warm the motor would often cut-out before going anywhere!

1940
Chevrolet Sedan

This is my Mum's Uncle, Alfred Myles (Snr)(RIP) car with his three girls Irene, Mavis and Audrey, sitting on the running-board.

After the big financial crash in 1932 nobody wanted to borrow one cent, and made sure there was cash to cover each purchase. I was given a lady's full-size bike for my seventh birthday and us kids only had three choices if we needed to go anywhere and that was on foot, by bike or horse. A car would only be used if we had to travel many miles, like going to town to shop, visiting my aunt's farm, attending a dance on Saturday night; or something special.

1930
MT MEE ROADWORKS

Courtesy of Moreton Bay Regional Libraries:

Road conditions at roadworks at Mt Mee, 1930 description shows the muddy and furrowed conditions of the roads during roadworks at Mt Mee.

Photo courtesy of Pine Rivers Library; Collector Jack Houghton

Morris Utility, Mt Mee

Notice Herb Myles' 3 children on board the Morris Utility, Robert and Donald with legs hanging over the side, and Janice behind them. Herb worked on the Mt Mee roadworks.

1932
DEPRESSION
Dad's Camp Site

This photo shows a typical Camp as dad moved around from place-to-place finding work. He was forced to leave his home on a pineapple farm at Glasshouse Mountains at 12 years of age when the family farm went broke during the Depression followed by a drought. Off he went on a pushbike with his swag, to find work and he did odd jobs, and learnt on the spot lots of practical life skills. Dad met a lot of people as he moved about. My Dad was a great survivor in the bush.

Dad would pitch his tent, tie his horse Toby up to a post, use the fence as a hanging rail to dry and air his gear. He would return at night to cook his tucker. Property owners would provide a horse, and some rations as required. Dad sometimes had his brother to help him and they would stay in that campsite until the odd jobs were completed. There were lots of odd jobs to be done on properties, like clearing land for cultivation, which would require skill with explosives, well sinking where explosives were also used, building sheds, painting, ring barking, shoeing horses, herding cattle and so on.

1940
Relaxation

Fishing in the Theodore River, near Cracow

This is Dad's brother Don on the left; Dad was rowing, and Mum and me at the back. (I look pretty cute peeping out under that big hat!)

1940
On the sand at Traveston, Queensland

Rita (me) at 9 months with Pam Allen. My Dad told me I ate all the sand at this beach!!

Kangaroo Shooting

Credit to TROVE:

William Sale's wife objected to Kangaroo shooting. His wife had accused him of preferring kangaroo shooting to her company, said William Lambheld Sale (36), Sergeant Dispenser in the A.I.F., in the Divorce Court today. Sale obtained a restitution order against his wife, Mona. He said she objected to him going on shooting trips with friends when they lived at Mildura between 1936 and 1939.

1939–1945
During the War

Courtesy of history.com:

> *Why did Australians want to enlist in World War II? Great Britain declared war on Germany on 3 September 1939. To help Britain, Australia formed the AIF to serve overseas. Aircrews from the RAAF and a number of RAN ships were also sent to fight for Britain.*

As early as September 1940 the State Munitions Board placed the first order for the manufacture of shells and grenade casings at Ipswich railway workshops. By 1941 armament industry machine tools were being manufactured at Toowoomba Foundry and Ipswich workshops were becoming a major source of munitions supply. Evans Deakin and Company in Brisbane and Walkers Limited of Maryborough were gearing up for the mass production of Australian-designed naval corvettes.

On 23 January 1942 the Japanese landed in New Guinea and the Solomon Islands. Rabaul was captured and Singapore fell on 15 February. The Prime Minister, John Curtin, described it as 'Australia's Dunkirk — the opening of the Battle of Australia'. 'Our honeymoon is finished, Curtin announced to the Australian people, "Now we must fight or work as never before."

This explains why so many locals from Ipswich, including my grandmother's family, were employed and learned trades at the Ipswich Railway Workshop.

The Department of Veteran Affairs report:

> *Thousands of women served in the armed forces in wider-ranging roles than nursing, to which they had traditionally been restricted. Many others undertook paid work in urban and rural industries, often while continuing to care for their homes and families. Children participated in fundraising events, knitted, and collected items for recycling.*

1942
Savills' Farm

Men who were on the land were not required to go to War, as they were a vital part of keeping supplies going. Our family was share-farming on a dairy about 10 miles out of Mungungo (just a little railway siding with a Post Office Store and Pub) while the owner of the farm enlisted in the War. My parents milked 35 cows by hand. It was some years later before Milking Machines were available, and affordable, which sure made the job easier; though jobs like leg roping the cow, and washing the udder were still necessary.

My Mum tying my bonnet. Apparently, we were off to a wedding.

This photo show so much of what I was trying to describe about the farm; the house, the tractor on the right, the tank and stand where the washing would be attended to, the dairy in the background to the left.

My Aunt Cass, visiting us at the farm, got off her horse and let me double-bank her daughter Bette on Apricot for a short ride.

Rationing

Google reports:

> *Food was rationed progressively from June 1942. Butter was the first item to be rationed, as Australia struggled to meet its commitments to Britain and the troops in the Pacific. Consumption was limited to one pound (454 grams) per adult per week, reduced to eight ounces in July 1943 and six ounces in 1944.*

Because so many personnel were engaged in the War there was a shortage of labour and commodities; therefore, each family was issued with coupons for food items, for example, tea, butter, rice, shoes, clothes, tobacco, etc. Garments were homemade and patched to keep them serviceable. There was coupon swapping amongst family and friends. I remember my dad making a roll your own cigarette using air mail writing paper. Thankfully, within a couple of years Dad quit smoking.

Butter Churning by Hand

My Dad would tie a billycan on the seat of the Tractor as he tilled the soil (this would save shaking the billy by hand) and that made the process of making butter quicker and easier. Hand churning was a slow and tiring process and sometimes took a couple of days to make a block of homemade butter.

Homemade Butter

There were no electrical appliances to make butter. Stale cream was easier to thicken. It was possible to shake each can several hours before the cream started "to turn" (where it would start separating the cream and the buttermilk). Mum would skim the cream off the house cow's milk to get extra cream for household use. Today cream is sold separately as a by-product of milk.

Methods of Cooking

Methylated Spirit Stove

This small methylated spirit stove was perfect for camping and heaps easier than boiling the billy or lighting the fire/stove.

Wood Stove

Every household had a wood stove, with some bigger and fancier than others. However, the stove served a few purposes; it was a heater for winter; it was a clothes dryer in wet weather; there was a kettle always ready for a cup of tea; just one more log on the fire would make it ready to cook the dinner, and bake a pudding or cake.

Ironing 1930s–1950s

Ma Pots Iron

Ironing was mostly only done on the best clothes for special occasions. Fortunately, I did not have a lot to do with the Ma Pots Irons that were heated by sitting them on a hot stove top. They were cast iron and heavy. I know they could leave a dirty black mark on good clothes and care had to be taken to rub them on a damp cloth before putting them on a garment, and if necessary, put a large handkerchief down to iron on top of that garment.

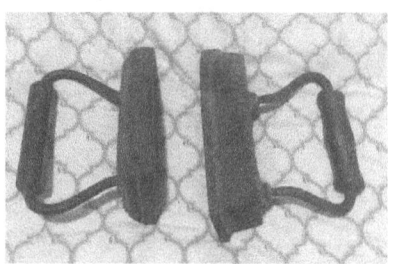

Image: Victorian Collections

Petrol Iron

Petrol Iron by Handi Works Pty Ltd

Ironing was for adults as this type of clothes iron used Shellite and that was flammable. Until electricity was connected and/or generators installed.

Image: Angelsea & District Historical Society

The Cream Lorry

This is not an original photo though it will give the reader a good idea of what it looked like. The cream carrier was a welcome sight, and delivered bread, fresh meat and mail and dropped off empty cream cans, to be filled for pickup on the next trip. We looked forward to this carrier coming 3 times a week. If we needed any supplies unexpectedly, the Carrier would collect parcels and supplies from the McGuigan's Store or Post Office which would save families a

trip. Pubs and Post Office Stores were very important as this was a way of communicating with the locals who called in for their mail and phone messages as they rode or drove home from shopping, mustering and so on. It was a slower pace these days, however the stresses were totally different, as people tried to figure out how to overcome the problems of no money, limited resources, pushing their imagination to the limit. People did help each other and would share their knowledge, stop if flagged down when travelling along the road, and given an errand to do. The people seemed to have an open mind in these times and were not shy to speak up and ask for help.

Flagging down for "help"

I remember clearly one day Mum, Dad and me were travelling from Cracow to Monto, and the old T-Model Ford broke down; Dad had diagnosed it was a crown wheel and pinion; stood beside the car on the side of the road and flagged down a passing motorist, who kindly gave me and Mum a lift to Monto while Dad waited for the car part to arrive.

Looking Back

The Mungungo Pub has never changed in 70 years. This Pub is still standing today and serving the local area with beers and meals. It caters for thirsty patrons during dances, the locals going past, and travellers calling in for a cold beer. These places really acted like a "bush telegraph" passing messages along the way from one caller to the other. At the back of the pub there stands a community hall and it would come alive on Saturday nights, and families (kids and all) would go to the dances, after travelling miles. These dances were important to me since it was not often, we got to interact with other families. During intermission (adults would have supper); the kids would slide around the very slippery floor. I remember getting a sprained wrist because us kids would squat down and be towed around by grabbing hands!

National Defence University finds:

The relationship between society and war is cyclical as war influences the language people use, how places are named, and encourages social changes. Despite being a mostly destructive force, war forces all individuals to contribute to their society: sometimes in non-traditional ways.

Washing or a Boil-up

Credit to Google:

Reckitt's Bag Blue laundry blue bags made in Australia by Reckitt and Colman (Australia) Ltd in about the 1930s and 1940s. The blueing process was used to whiten material made yellow from soap and age. After washing, a 'blue bag' was dipped in a clean tub of cold water. Each piece of clothing was turned inside out and plunged into the water, then rinsed. 'Blue bags' were also handy as a remedy for bee stings.

My Mum used to make Bar Soap (yes, there was a recipe for soap being shared around) and the newly made bar of soap would sit on the tank stand in the hot sun to dry. The main ingredients for Bar Soap were Tallow and Caustic Soda. There was only one tank and water was scarce. To get the wash started, we had two kerosine tins put onto an open fire that sat on two iron bars; each tin would have cold water in it, with one for the towels and sheets, and the other for our work clothes. Mum would poke the clothes up and down while they were very hot, and being careful not to let the water overflow onto the fire underneath. Once the clothes were clean Mum had two sticks that would be used to transfer the hot clothes out into a big tub for rinsing. We had a wash stand for the tubs situated near the tap. Clothes were hand wrung, and plunged into "blue water" hand rung then pegged onto a line supported in the middle with a prop.

Wireless

The life style was very simple. Often the reception was awful and it was about the only way to get news about the War, or important events.

Our wireless was a lovely piece of furniture. It had this huge cabinet, inside were valves, and if one of those "blew" nothing would work.

Gramophone Turntable

Songs were played by placing records on a Gramophone turntable, (HMV was the known brand). Many families had a hand wound gramophone and a great collection of records. It was necessary to hand wind the gramophone (a small square box shape with a lift up lid); the idea was that, as the spring tightened by the winding, the music would play. It was sort of like a wind-up toy idea. As the springs wound-down the music would play slower and slower until it sounded like a drawl.

Neighbours

The nearest neighbour was three miles away. The day-to-day chores consumed the day. Horses were the main mode of transport. Messages were often delivered by the Cream Lorry Driver. Some properties had a Party-line where as many as six families would share the phone line.

There was a limited amount of everything, e.g., fruit, vegetables, money, fuel, commodities, visitors and entertainment.

Race Meetings

I remember when I visited my uncle and aunt's farm, each Saturday afternoon would be race meeting day, and my uncle would keep in contact with his sister (Ede Williams) on the party line, and it was all about racing form and a few bets would be placed. I remember clearly the instructions "Keep quiet, you kids."

Farm Machinery

Farm machinery was scarce and anything we had was old and needed fixing before use. Mostly the fields were ploughed with a single furrow plough pulled behind a draught horse.

We once borrowed a Fordson Tractor to plough and planted corn, and cotton. Limited rainfall made growing crops and ploughing hard work.

We left this farm after the War ended.

Being Bored Makes for Mischief

During the war as a 5-year-old, and not having any siblings at this stage, I did not like being at the dairy while milking was being done, especially in cold or wet weather and I would look for things to occupy my time.

Smoking

If it was wet or cold, I would not go to the cow yard to bail up, and instead I would get up to mischief by myself at the house. Dad smoked in the early days, and during the War years, with rationing and lack of money, had to roll his own, and there were no cigarette papers (zig zags), and he would use the airmail writing paper; cut it into pieces, ready to roll up the tobacco. Getting the bits of paper to stick down was an art, and Dad would bite the paper, well that is what I reckoned he was doing, together with a bit of spit,  making bite marks, to form a tacky surface. So, I thought while Mum and Dad were milking the cows, I would roll a smoke using corn tassel and newspaper. I got a chair and sat in front of the firebox and lit up the end with the hot coals. I didn't do a neat job this time, and a bit of paper stuck out so I lit the ugly looking cigarette I had made, and "whoof" it flared up, and singed my eyebrows, and hairs on my forearm. My parents did not say a word!! I could even smell the singeing hair!

Peanut Paste

This particular day I was waiting for Mum and Dad to come from the cow yard and I thought I would get into the peanut paste for a quick feed, while nobody was looking. I ate half a bottle by the spoonful. I got as sick as a dog, and did not eat peanut paste again for 25 years, and then it was with honey on it.

Slippers

For my birthday I got a lovely pair of felt slippers. I wore them outside in the wet grass, which was not allowed, so then thought I would (destroy the evidence) and fix that by putting them in the oven (while the fire was going) and when Mum opened the oven door hours later my lovely slippers were black and charred. I said to Mum "that's what Dad does to dry his boots". Of course, his were leather, and he made sure the stove was only warm. Good try — bad idea.

TOUGH TIMES

When I was born in 1938 things were still very tough, and families headed to the gold fields during the gold rush to find work.

A Luxury Feed

A wood duck, gunned down and dragged out of the local water hole by the dog, then plucked, gutted, stuffed and roasted in the camp oven with roast spuds/sweet potato and pumpkin.

Fruit and Veggies

Often fruit and vegetables were local produce or wild bush grown, and picked at random, e.g. gooseberries, raspberries, oranges, and mandarins usually grown alongside the cattle troughs or wells/windmill, as well as tomatoes and pumpkin. Other supplies, including fresh meat, were often given to the local squatters by property owners, in return for some toil, e.g., fixing a fence, branding cattle, slaughtering, welding, well sinking, painting etc. Dad was not a qualified mechanic though he was often required to fix an engine. A kind of barter system.

Recipes

Damper

Ingredients	Method
2 cups self-raising flour water 1 teaspoon salt dried fruit for choice	Mix all ingredients together to make a wet dough. Tip onto floured alfoil. Shape into a large sausage. Roll up loosely and seal ends. Dig a hole in hot coals and drop damper in and cover with coals. No fire on top. Leave 20 minutes. Dig out and unwrap.

Pumpkin Scones

Ingredients	Method
½ cup of sugar 2¾ cups self raising flour 1 cup cooked mashed pumpkin 1 egg 1 Tablespoon butter pinch of salt	Cream sugar and butter. Add egg and pumpkin. Fold in the sifted flour. Roll out to half inch thickness and cut with scone cutter. Bake in a hot oven.

Main Meals

Credit to Google:

> *Families also kept eggs fresher and storing them for longer periods of time with the pointy side down in a rack, and the rack inserted into a pail filled with waterglass (a liquid mixture of sodium silicate). Waterglass sealed the pores of the eggs and allowed them to stay fresh.*

The main meal was corn beef, damper and spuds. Anything requiring refrigeration would keep fresh a lot longer if "corned". Corned silverside would be pumped with a brine solution to help preserve it, and then rolled in coarse salt. Eggs would be put into an old cream can with a preserving liquid agent (it felt a bit slimy). Food was stored in a gauze enclosed hanging safe; larger items in an area/enclosure with a concrete floor. In the city there was an Iceman going from house to house with his horse and cart selling large blocks of ice.

Breakfast

The word still comes to mind, "What's for breakfast?" and the answer would be, "Lizard's lips on toast" or "Eggs scattered like ya brains." Dad's sense of humour put a whole different slant on the day.

Toast

A slice of toast was made by suspending a slice of bread on a fork over the open fire or over the hot coals. Many times the toast would catch alight. Singed and burnt toast was common; and if you did not like burnt toast it was easy to scratch the burnt bits off and then spread vegemite or honey to make it attractive.

Billy Tea

When I worked in the forest with my dad, the billy was boiled on an open fire hanging on a stick, and the tea leaves thrown in at boiling point. Dad would not measure anything except put sugar in the tea cup by shaking the bottle, as well as stirring his tea with a twig.

This photo was taken on a day trip, travelling by car to visit brother Keron in hospital.

Keeping Food Cool

Often a hole was dug in the creek bed where it was cool and surrounded by small rocks and this would help stop the butter from turning to oil. Meat was corned (coarse salt) to preserve it and hung in a wire safe to keep the flies away or wrapped in a cheesecloth rag.

Honey

Usually, the honey was robbed from hives found in the trees. The wax honeycomb was then put into a large cloth, a bit like when a plum pudding was made and placed in a cheese cloth, then tied with a piece of rope or wire and hung on a tree branch to drain into a container.

LIGHTS

Carbide light

This light was perfect for night fishing, or to provide light when shooting around dams when it was pitch dark.

The advantage of this light was it had no glass globe and could withstand water and rain. Comparing to the current times, torches have been a replacement as well as mobile phones.

Hurricane Light

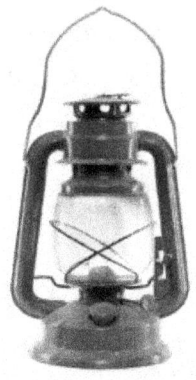

The hurricane light was durable, strong, and reliable and easy to light with no fuss, making it very practical. As more demand was put on consumers, improved models of household lights were produced. Campers used this type light for many years.

Tilly Light

The Tilly was used as an inside light and would mostly be hanging over the kitchen table as it would light up the room and stay there until bed time. It ran on kerosene and if the light got dim it meant it needed priming (pumping) or was lacking fuel.

PREDATORS AND PREY

Snakes

Non-venomous — Carpet Snake

From Kidszone.ws:

> *Many people find it surprising that the largest and the scariest snakes can be afraid of anything, but it is true. While they are young, they are easy prey to many birds and mammals but when they are older and larger, they have humans to fear.*

Image: Ann Ludlow

Venomous — Eastern Brown and Black

Everyone was always on the lookout for snakes, not because they would attack, but because they were hard to see, since they would hide in or under a log or sheet of tin. If you saw them, it was easy to let them crawl away; however, if a foot or hand accidentally touched them, they could strike. The rule was to roll a log or sheet of tin over with your foot before picking it up with your hands. Covered in boots/shoes were also a good preventative.

Venomous — Red Bellied Black

They like water, they can swim, they are curious. One day at my beach house, I was sitting in the outdoor area talking on the phone, and I sensed something, and this red bellied black crawled around the corner and gave me an awful fright. Another time my son was playing his guitar in the outdoor area and a red belly black was under the table near his feet. I found these snakes to be more friendly if you left them alone.

NUISANCES WHEN CAMPING ON SITE

Goannas

Goannas and possums were a pest as they would rummage through the tent at night for a feed, knocking over things as they went, as well as taking a bite or leaving something half eaten. Goannas would rip up the kangaroo skins that were pegged out and ruin them for sale at the market.

Possums

Possums could be pets and hang around the camp. One afternoon this baby possum that Dad had rescued was all cuddled up in my arms, then just looked up at me, and took a bite of my chin!

On the Spot Nursing Aid

In the country areas Doctors and Hospitals were not easy to access due to the long distances to travel; the dirt roads were narrow and rough. In an emergency a horse could be used when professional treatment was required.

First Aid

Cuts were cleaned and wrapped in an old torn up singlet with a piece of old white calico sheet over the top.

Finger stalls were the best for keeping wounds clean. For bandaging a strip would be ripped/cut off an old sheet, with a 6-inch split at the end, a knot tied so it could be fastened around and tied off. Peroxide was used for cleaning. Iodine was also used to kill bacteria in 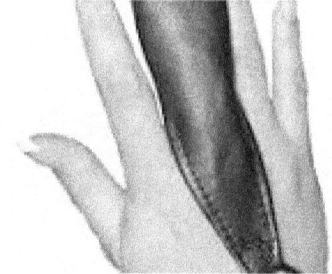 case of infection. I had my own small axe — it was probably more like a tomahawk, and I put a gash in my shin (the scar is still there). My Mum was very patient and kind with her attention to injuries and could handle blood, and clean things up as required. Her ability to make a fingerstall out of an old scrap was invaluable when cuts to fingers and toes were exposed to dirty conditions. We never threw a clean piece of cloth away and used singlets to make bandaging, and old sheets to wrap around wounds.

Mum would fuss about the little kangaroos who were not yet old enough to survive in the world; she would get the chicken hatchlings and put them near the oven of the stove to keep warm.

Medical treatment was almost unheard of. Earache was treated with warm olive oil and a cotton wool plug. Splinters or bits of wood were dug out with a pointed sharpened pocket knife, and any trimming of skin would be trimmed with the cut-throat razor. Dad would sharpen a pocket knife until he could shave the hairs on his arms. Boils or infections were treated with a heated poultice made from a concoction of fruit, veggie scraps, bread and/or castor oil, plus washing soda, as well as sugar/honey, and/or conge boy leaves. Cleansing was done depending what was on hand; things like iodine, peroxide, permeates of potash (we called it Condy's Crystal) mentholated spirits, and kerosene. My Mum had a big burn mark on her thigh where a hot poultice was applied to treat a boil. It sure killed the germs and pulled the skin off as well. Strangely, burns would have butter rubbed onto them.

Bites

As a kid a scorpion bit me on the toe. These critters resembled a small prawn with pincers on their tail. They live under old logs on the ground. Fortunately, that bush treatment must have worked since I am here to tell the tale!

Centipedes

These can also be found under logs, old dead wood and hidden places on the ground. They are reddish in colour, and have at least a thousand legs! These nasties are quite poisonous.

IMPROVISING AND FLEXIBILITY FOR COOLING

Cooling

Credit to Google:

> *Thomas Masters patented a method of making ice in 1843; he used the heat absorption of a chemical mixture to create ice, but required new chemicals each time ice was made.*

1952 ESKY produced by Malley's

The Esky was a boost for picnics and outdoor activities; also, great if there was a black-out.

Portable coolers soon became a staple item for camping, trips to the beach, and picnics.

1953 Ice Coolers

Google reports:

In 1953 Richard C. Laramy received a U.S. patent for his invention of a portable ice chest for storing and refrigerating foods and the like. The Ice Cooler is insulated to prevent ice melting quickly.

There was a commercial operation in Brisbane called The Ice Works, that delivered large blocks of ice in the city areas. When I came to the city in the early 1950's my aunt would get an ice delivery by horse and cart where she would buy a large solid block produced at the Ice Works, and it would fit into an Ice Chest. These early inventions were mostly of benefit to the people in the city.

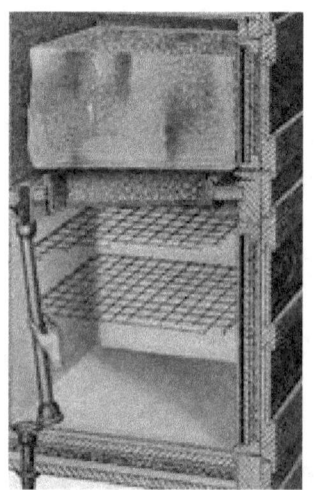

Ice Box

An icebox is portable, a compact non-mechanical refrigerator that held a large block of ice and could be carried by two people which meant it held more food and would fit into a vehicle making it very versatile.

In the country my Aunt Cass had a hole in the ground under the house with cement walls for cold storage.

Often the farmers dug a hole in the shallows of the creek bed for keeping butter so it did not end up as a grease/oil patch and go rancid.

Refrigeration

Google reports:

> *In Australia, Edward Hallstrom (later Sir Edward) produced his first kerosene-powered refrigerator in his Sydney backyard.*
>
> *In the small country towns and on Australian outback farms kerosene refrigerators made by Hallstrom's from 1928 were used where electricity was not available.*

1958 Silent Knight Refrigerator

Manufactured by Hallstrom. It was a household name in refrigerators. Initially these refrigerators would make a bit of a shuddering noise as the compressor cut in and out.

1945
September 2ⁿᴰ Ended the War

The day Peace was declared, the whole districts went to town in Monto, having big celebrations, and there was marching in the streets and drums banging, etc. I had not seen some of my uncles for years.

The end of the War brought about happiness where men returned home to their families, lovers got married to their brides, Army Disposal Stores opened up selling off excess army jackets, etc. Here are some photos of my family taken during the War.

1943: Uncle Roly Myles outside his camp in New Guinea. He got one minor injury when a gunshot grazed his shoulder blade.

Rocky Creek Memorial Park

Credit to rc.qld.gov.au:

> *A few kilometres along the Kennedy Highway north of Tolga the Rocky Creek Memorial Park is situated on the 2/2nd Australian General Hospital laundry and medical stores site. During WW2 the Tablelands*

area became the biggest military base in Australia with camps in Tinaroo, Karai, Atherton, Wongabel, Herberton, Wondecla, Ravenshoe and Mt Garnett. Rocky Creek was the site of the biggest military hospital in the southern hemisphere that had 3,000 beds and treated over 60,000 patients from 1943 to 1945.

The things that happened in the war were not talked about by the returned soldiers. This information has come to hand by Carol Watson who mentioned camping at Rocky Point Memorial Park; then it came to light that Uncle Alf Myles said he was an Ambulance Driver at this hospital, and I was told he was an Orderly. It was likely he was both.

Uncle Alf Myles, one of Mum's older brothers ventured overseas after the war ended and I did not see him for seven years. He was a keen musician and played the bugle, and at his funeral at 99.5 years of age, the RSL gave him a big "send-off".

Don Hansen, my dad's youngest brother, returned to Cracow where his bride to be (Queenie) was waiting for him.

Uncle Stan Ludlow and Dorothy Myles Marry

After the War was over there were weddings galore as couples "tied the knot" in celebration. Here is my Aunt Doll (Dorothy Myles) marrying her lover Stanley Ludlow after he returned from service.

Back row: Alf Myles, Arnold Krause, Stan Ludlow, Dolly Myles, Enid Myles, Jean Russell.

Front row: Flower girls: Beryl Krause, Rita Paulos (Me)

1946
Howies' Farm

Andy Howie was a returned soldier who needed a break and my parents looked after the farm while he had a holiday. The photo below is not an original photo of that farm but very similar in its features.

Cow Yard

Cows were herded into the yards by dogs or on horseback.

Credit to Donald Myles

Cow Bails

Credit to Margaret List (Myles) for the photo of their bails on their farm.

Explaining the details of these cow bails where the cows would be leg-roped, teats washed while in the bails, the milking machine cups would be attached by suction onto the cow's teat, sending the fresh milk shooting up to the pipes, where there was a flask showing the amount of milk flow (a lot of milk coming from the cow or little). Then once the milk entered the pipes it would be forced to the huge vat and then directed into a large separator that had two spouts, and this would separate the cream from the milk which was channelled into two cream cans (one skim milk, and one cream). The by-products of the dairy and farm cultivation was used to feed the animals on the farm. For example, milk for the poddies who were now not sucking their mothers. Once the mothers calved, they soon joined the milking herd again. Cream was the real-life blood of the farm as it was then transported by cream lorry to the butter factory.

The farmer then waited for his cream cheque showing him how well his herd were doing, and what level of butterfat they were producing. Attached to the dairy was a closed in room to house the machinery required for separating (always locked to keep the poddies from helping themselves). This room also stored the cream cans, and is where washing the vats, separator and accessories after each milking period took place. Our catch cry when we went to town or visiting was, "Got to be home by 4pm, to start milking." The cows would start making their way to the yards of the dairy ready for a handful of chaff, chew their cud and get their udder emptied. Their job was done allowing them to find their camping spot on the flats for the night. Now we know why our forebears had strong forearms and hands like paws!

Milking Machine Teat Suction Cups

Howies' farm owner had milking machines installed and this was a great advantage and saved hand emptying of buckets of milk into the vat. It also meant it was possible to milk a bigger herd in the same amount of time.

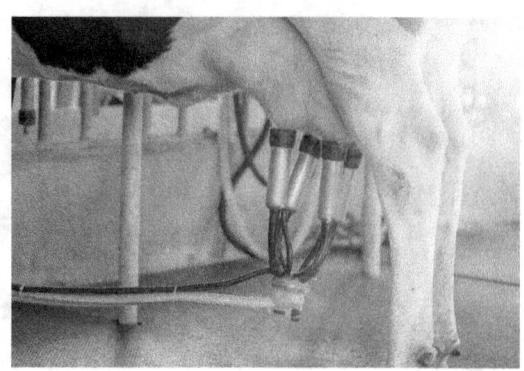

1998: Herringbone Sheds for Milking Cows

As dairying became more commercialised, and crops like lucerne were cultivated to feed the cows which increased the volume of milk produced. Having 100 cows to milk morning and evening, these up-market style of milking machines were invaluable.

Image: Carol Watson — Watson Farm at Bendigo, Victoria

Calves

Credit to Donald Myles for this photo.

Calves were taken from their mother very early and hand fed from a bucket. The mother cow would then join the herd being milked at the dairy. Often, we would put two poddy calves coupled together with a strap and chain with a swivel (the cow's calf plus another) to suck the one cow to keep the milk supply down and, at the same time, to rear one extra beast. Milk could not be used immediately after a cow had a calf, like humans, there is a short period until it became nice and white in colour, and the milk starts to flow. Without good care in the early stages of calving problems like mastitis could occur where the udder of the mother cow gets hot and hard, and sometimes it would curdle the milk making it unsuitable for use.

After feeding each poddy, myself and Bette and Fay would throw a little froth on them to signify they'd had their fill.

Heifers

The young heifers would go into a special paddock and be introduced to the stud bull; this would ultimately increase the number of poddies as well as the number of beasts.

Veterinarians

Credit to Google with an extract *The Department at War* outlining how difficult it was to provide professional staff from 1940 to 1950:

> *The war had a huge impact on the agricultural industry limiting the availability of professional staff, veterinarians, and inspectors.*
>
> *Veterinary education, training, and employment shifted to support military needs in wartime. Conflicts around the world, including World War I, relied on millions of horses, dogs, and food-producing animals to supply armies. Wartime disruptions, and the movement of so many animals, sparked outbreaks of diseases that challenged animal owners, healers, and veterinarians. The use of horsepower declined in industrialized areas, depriving veterinarians of their most important patients. Many turned instead to livestock and food production. National campaigns against bovine tuberculosis, brucellosis, and other zoonoses employed many veterinarians. Others worked on vaccines and therapeutics in biomedical research. With the outbreak of World War II, ethical questions troubled veterinarians who contributed to the development of biological weapons. Rebuilding the world's food production systems after the war stimulated international veterinary cooperation and incorporated new tools, such as*

antibiotics. Veterinarians also helped make intensive animal production ("factory farming") possible by controlling diseases, while more and more vets in wealthier areas treated companion animals (pets).

This article explains why Vets were not heard of. Besides, with a limited number of staff, and the vast areas to be serviced, it was not practical. Fortunately, all animals were treated on the spot with injections behind the shoulder blades or the rump by the farm workers.

Sick Cows

If the cow got sick or too poor in the drought, especially after calving, and was weak, it was sometimes necessary to nurse them back to good health. If the beast got down and could not get up a sling would be made out of corn bags, and slung under their belly, supported by a couple of posts/supports, to help hold them on their feet, because once a sick cow got down on the ground it was often impossible for them to stand up and it was better to have them on their hooves. If the cows did not recover, they were shot, dragged down the paddock and burnt. This would prevent bacteria spreading.

Engines

The milking machines used a motorised engine as well as the tractors, slashers, harvesters, and irrigation pump. The choice was horse power (draft horses) or fuel that was purchased in very large drums and hand pumped into small drums for convenient use.

1946
LUDLOW'S FARM, KALPOWAR

Credit to Peter Williams for the aerial photograph of the property and surrounds. Ludlow's house can be seen at the rear of the photo; and our house in Kalpowar, where we ultimately lived, is the building at the front of this aerial picture.

Our family was given the opportunity to live at Aunty Doll and Uncle Stan's farm (Mum's sister and her husband). They were married following the end of the War and moved to this property at Kalpowar. There was a grain/corn shed, not shown in the photos; it was 100 yards to the right of the main house.

Ludlow's Old Farm House

There was a huge corn crop growing in the paddock to the right of the fence when we moved into the shed. The dilapidated fence around the cultivation paddock is seen in this photo (80 years later).

This farm's location made my schooling a lot easier to access, as it was about two miles from the local town of Kalpowar and the State School. I would walk or ride my bike, over two creek crossings, and a dirt road (as shown in the aerial picture). Horses or bicycles were the mode of transport as the motor cars were only used when the family went to Monto, or a family outing. I liked it here and I would wonder up to the dairy after school and chase the cows into the bails ready for milking; then after milking, when the milk had been separated, it was time to feed the separated milk to the poddies and pigs.

Below are some recent photos of Ludlow's farm, where it shows that once the next generation had watched their parent's milk twice daily and work seven days a week, they soon transferred to raising beef cattle. This meant some beneficiaries were absentee land-owners. Unfortunately, once dairy farming ceased, and the old folks moved to retirement, the places deteriorated as a lot of the buildings like cow yards, poddy pens and pig stys were no longer needed.

During our recent cousin's visit to the district, Margaret (Myles) List is making friends with one of the old farm horses that looks to be in its retirement.

The following two photos show some out buildings as well as superseded machinery.

1948
Wash Day Inventions

Hand washing was not exactly an easy job; some people had washboards to rub the clothes on to remove dirty marks. Subsequently my dad made a plunger for the old copper. Progress was slow but sure! Dad made a plunger for the old copper, and much later he fitted a hand turned roller that made it easier to wring the clothes out before hanging them on the line.

Hand Washing Machine

This is a hand operated washing machine with a plunger to manually pump up and down to agitate the water and suds to clean the clothes.

Unless power was available none of the semi-automatic or automatic machines were useable.

Hand Operated Wringer

My Dad mounted one of these hand turned wringer/rollers on the side of the concrete wash tubs.

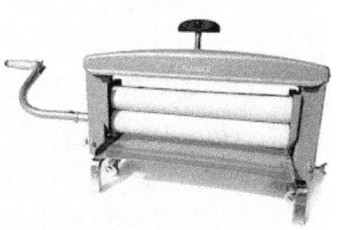

Concrete Wash Tubs

A spare wash tub is still a boost today whether concrete or stainless steel, since there are always shoes to clean, paint brushes to wash, and those dirty jobs to be done.

1948: A Twin-tub Washing Machine

Also known as a semi-automatic washing machine, is a type of machine that has two separate tubs, one for washing, and one for spinning clothes. Even today, in spite of the automatic washing machines, some families have this simple wash and spin machine for use.

Pope/Simpson Electric Washing Machine

1961: hand washing.

I washed by hand for a year. Then this complete machine was affordable.

1945: The Hills Hoist

Credit to Google:

> *Developed in Adelaide, South Australia by World War II veteran Lance Hill. His reason for this initiative was the overcrowding of his yard.*

Country folk had plenty of room and trees to attach their line and were not in a hurry to changeover. This hoist was multi-purpose, as kids loved to use it as a gym and swing!

Land Clearing

Felling Hoop Pine

In the early days of moving to Kalpowar dad became a forestry contractor cutting hoop pine. He would ride off into the scrub very early each day to cut down hoop pine trees using a cross-cut saw, hand operated. At the weekend he would sharpen the saw, axe and tools ready for another hard week. In his spare time, he would help my uncle on the farm with odd jobs like fencing, ploughing and clearing land.

Cultivation

To clear a paddock ready for crops was a big project as trees, stumps, roots, and shale had to be removed before cultivation could begin. Explosives, by the use of gelignite, were used to blow the stumps/roots out of the ground. My Dad was able to do this by drilling a large hole into the tree roots at the base of the stump, using a hand turned auger. This is where a piece of gelignite would be plugged, with a fuse attached, and once lit, it would give the operator time to go for cover behind a tree in case the explosion sent fragments into the air. Dad would call out, "Timber!" and anyone within ear-shot would run and hide behind a large tree.

Ploughing

Credit Thought Co: Plow advances and farm tractors:

> *From the single plow, advances were made to two or more plows fastened together, allowing for more work to be done with approximately the same amount of manpower (or animal-power). Another advance was the sulky plow, which allowed the Plowman to ride, rather than walk. Such Plows*

were in use as early as 1844. The next step forward was to replace animals that pulled the plows with traction engines. By 1921, farm tractors were both doing the work better and pulling more plows—50 horsepower engines could pull 16 plows, harrows, and a grain drill. Farmers could thus perform the three operations of ploughing, harrowing, and planting all at the same time and cover 50 acres or more in a day.

Horse Drawn Single Furrow Plough

Here is a single-furrow plough tilling the soil; it is being controlled by a person who holds the reins to control the horses, the plough handles to control the plough, to make sure the furrows were in a straight line.

My aunt Doll had a vegetable patch and Dad used a single furrow plough and draft horse to prepare the soil for planting. It was about an acre of ground on the bend of the creek. It was a hard job as the plough would bounce off roots and stones and Dad was swaying from side to side trying to keep the plough upright. Draft Horses were used to pull heavy loads.

These working horses are not bred for speed, and used for their strength. When trying to identify these horses, take a look at their solid build and the size of their hooves. They have lots of hair growing around their fetlocks and are very sure-footed animals.

Tractor Drawn Plough

Farming became a lot easier once motorised engines came into the world.

Today, ploughs are not used nearly as extensively as before. This is due in large part to the popularity of minimum tillage systems designed to reduce soil erosion and conserve moisture.

New Pony

Unfortunately, I had to leave Tommy behind when we left the old farm. My Grandpa had given me a nice little foal, creamy in colour, which Dad tamed by handling and spending a couple of days breaking him in (training) so he could be harnessed and rode without bucking and jumping about. I liked a frisky horse but he was a bit cunning, and if he was not continually worked would get smart and try to pig-root, and once tried to rub me up against a tree when yarding horses.

My First Buster off Creamy

Creamy was my very own pony. This day I was invited to a party, and Dad said before he went to work, "Be careful, he is a bit fresh, harness him, walk him around, let him get used to the crupper and girth, check them a couple of times before you get on him." I got all dressed, hat and all, ready to go. I put my foot in the stirrup, swung my leg over the saddle, and as soon as my bottom hit the seat Creamy started fidgeting around, and kept walking and stomping, and silly me not thinking, was only a few yards away from the clothesline; and while I am concentrating on Creamy's nonsense he went under the clothesline, and off I came backwards and landed on the ground. Creamy ran away saddle, bridle and all. My Uncle Stan Ludlow heard the commotion and came to the rescue, caught him, got on him in the creek bed of sand, kicked him in the ribs many times, and said, "Buck, you bugger," and of course Creamy could not lift his legs in the sand, and with my uncle's weight on him, he had to surrender. He was a gem but a little devil! I loved him just the same!

Our lives were about surviving in the bush and using our dairy/farm skills to our advantage. The choices were stay at home and be miserable and bored or to be involved in whatever was happening around us and learning and doing what we could. Staying at home was very boring.

The Army Disposal Stores

These stores sold lots of clothes and Mum ordered me an overcoat (Small Men's Green Army Waist Coat), which was the only warm jacket I had. It sure was all-purpose. I had one pair of shoes for best, and a pair of sandshoes for tennis, otherwise I was barefooted, even in winter. All the kids at school were in the same boat, and our feet would get cracks from the wet grass, and the soles of our feet felt like leather. In fact, we would hardly feel a prickle, and we had competitions to see who could go over the most prickles without getting a bindy-eye in their feet. In rainy weather we used a corn bag, pushed one corner in to form a pixie shape on the top as a raincoat, especially for outside jobs. The pixie shape fitted over our head, letting the rest of the bag hanging down the back to keep our bottom dry.

Snigging Logs, Kalpowar Forest

Kalpowar State Forest

Credit Queensland Government, Department Environment and Science:

In the foothills of the Burnett Range, Kalpowar State Forest protects a mosaic of forests. Patches of dense rainforest with towering hoop pines remain between open eucalypt forests and hoop pine plantations. More than 150 plant species occur in the hoop pine rainforest which was first logged in 1918. Fireclay Road got its name from local clay used to make bricks before the plantations were established here. The first hoop pine plantation of about 12ha was developed in 1934 and the last available area was planted in 1991.

Pushing Scrub at Kalpowar Forestry

This is my dad pushing scrub with a Bulldozer to build roads through the forest to enable workers to plant new seedlings, as well as contractors to cut and haul timber to the Railway Yards. Building fire breaks was also part of the care of the plantation.

During school holidays Uncle Don Hansen visited with a couple of cousins and we drove into the scrub to visit Dad to have lunch. This picture shows Mum at the front, my sister Fay behind her, Uncle Don to the right, two boys, and others hidden by the cabin of the dozer.

Cutting the Logs

Men usually worked in pairs making it easier to manage a huge log. Two guys would see-saw a six-foot cross-cut saw, or one man would manage the job. If one man could log five of these trees a day that would be a good tally.

Loading the Logs via a Ramp

Hauling Logs

Dad with the Maple Leaf Truck loading logs, via the ramp, using a crow bar. Railway wagons would be shunted off the main railway line, waiting for the logs to arrive into the railway yard, to be transported to the saw mill.

Rita helping hook up logs for a bob a day

Labour and Housing Shortage

It was about this time that there was a labour shortage and the Forestry employed lots of Italian and Baltic migrants. The Forestry Department built tent like barracks out towards the scrub for single men. The Forestry also erected married quarters to attract families to the area; these structures were constructed using weather boards on the bottom half, canvas on the top, with a fly over the top, to protect the dwellers from heat, wind and rain.

The attendance at the school rocketed to 50 kids and only one teacher.

1957–1958
A Tour of a Farmer's Dairy
Dayboro, Queensland

Herbie Myles (Uncle Jack's son) purchased a farm at Dayboro (about 50 km from the Brisbane City); it is a good example of a well-planned and organised farm.

The Farm set up and outbuildings

Photo credit to Donald Myles

Any farm that had a cottage for a "share farmer" as well as a main homestead to use as residence was a pretty good deal.

In this photo there is the main house on the left with a small enclosure for saddles and bridles and other horse gear. At the back on the left is a small saw mill. There is also a car shed and "dunny" and a dog kennel at the back. Behind the lump of trees (mango tree). in the middle of the photo is the share farmers cottage.

Cow Yards

Here is the front left of the dairy with cow bails and milking machines. Note the huge fig tree behind.

This photo shows a different aspect of the dairy from the far right.

Pooper Scoop

Using what was a horse drawn "Pooper-Scoop" behind a tractor, needing a person to hold the shafts stable while moving forward to collect the cow dung.

An Aberdeen Angus Bull protecting his heifers

Breeding Paddock

Cows heavily in-calf waiting for their calves to be born

Journey Through Education

Primary School — Pre-Kalpowar

Looking back, it feels as though I learnt more out of school hours than during school hours. My Primary schooling was for reading, writing and arithmetic.

1943 — Grade 1: Correspondence

My first year was Correspondence lessons and my Mum tried to teach me and it really did not work out very well. My Aunt Cass who lived on a farm about a mile over the hill would help out sometimes and that worked out heaps better for me. My Mum and I could not work together, and my Aunt Cass used to do a few lessons to help. I could walk to her place carrying my books in a sugar bag.

1944 — Grade 2: Riding to Clonmel SS from Savill's Farm

Ye olde Clonmel School

It was 8 miles from the farm to the Clonmel State School. As I was still a bit "little" Dad would accompany me to a neighbouring farm, owned by Mr & Mrs Dick Warren, and I would ride on with their kids to the Clonmel State School and we would join more kids riding to school as we went. My horse was Krombit, a quiet, steady footed, solid gelding; not fast or flash but trustworthy; he was probably a half-draft (half draft and half saddle horse). The school had a horse paddock where all the kids from the district left their horses during school, and the saddles and bridles would be stacked under the school shed. The big boys (12 years old) from the school would help the younger ones catch and saddle their horses to go home. I could not reach the horses head to put the bridle on or get on Krombit without first standing on a stump or log.

It is easy to see why getting Krombit ready for my return trip home was so difficult! I looked like a "pimple on a pumpkin" on Krombit.

Saddling my Horse

Imagine how long I would take to get ready for home after school if I had to do it all by myself, e.g., Step 1, was to throw the reins around the horse's neck and lead him to a log or stump; Step 2, stand up, and reach to fit the bridle over his head; Step 3, fit the bit into his mouth. If he threw his head in the air I would scold him, if he behaved, he got a pat and cuddle. Sometimes I would clamber on by jumping off a log, and grabbing his mane to pull myself on bareback to ride back to the school building. Since I was expected home before dark, accompanied halfway, the older boys would come to the rescue. This afternoon a Scholarship boy "legged" me on the horses back with his hand/arm sling and threw me right over to the other side, as I was supposed to grab Krombit's mane to steady my landing on his back. Thinking about it now, he probably meant it!

All of my Primary years were spent at one Teacher schools, where we had an open learning type of environment. The teacher had five to seven kids in each class, all in the same schoolroom, and the teacher would go from class to class. I spent many hours on the school verandah in front of a chart with a pointing stick repeating my schoolwork, e.g. addition tables chart, spelling chart, good manners chart.

Later in Year 3

It was back to Clonmel State School, as we moved to another returned soldier's farm which was only about 3 miles from the previous farm but it was in better shape, better house, better cow bales, and milking machines, pig yards, and some crops. This farm was closer to the Primary school I had attended previously. The house was situated away from the main road, and we were on the side of the hill overlooking the road to the neighbour's property. My best memories are about me hitting a

tennis ball against the verandah wall; I got given a pet goat, as well as a new horse Tommy to ride to school.

My New Horse Tommy

My new horse was loaned to me by the neighbour whose name was Tommy. This time it was a pony, and he was younger and flasher, I called him Tommy. He became my mate. I could catch him and harness him myself. I didn't need the stumps and logs to get on his back. We bonded well; I would feed him thistles and a handful of milo (grain) after school, and that would make him frisky.

School Dentist

Our school had a visit by a mobile dental unit, transported to the school for one week. I went once, for an inspection, and I knew I had holes in my teeth, and fillings would be necessary. I got really scared. Why not? They drilled holes by hand with a foot treadle drill! I would not go to school and said I felt sick (with the thought of it and did not explain that to Mum though). Mum said, "If you don't go to school after 2 days, you have to go to the Doctor."

1946: After the War Ended

1946 Cracow State School

At this time, I had a short six weeks attending the Cracow State School, as my family visited my dad's parents.

Kangaroo Shooting

Things started to change as soldiers arrived back to their families and farms. This also affected our family as we were share farming or caretaking farms for a couple of guys who were enlisted in the War. Dad had to make up his mind what he was going to do, and he decided to visit his parents at Cracow and to catch up with Uncle Don who was returning from the War. The prices of kangaroo skins increased and a short stint of moving about the west might work for a few months. It also was like a holiday as me and Mum were also able to go bush for a while.

Yes, I was supposed to be at school and I was enrolled at the Cracow State School and stayed with Grandma and Grandpa Hansen. Once the Christmas school holidays came along, I got a chance to join the kangaroo shooting adventure. The 'roo skins were the goal.

'Roo Shooting Trip

It was only a short stay at Cracow and Mum and Dad came back to collect me. So off we went, and set up camp close to a creek on a cattle property, and occasionally visited the property homestead for supplies. This was different indeed. I rode my bike when looking for kangaroos that grazed close to our Camp, and then I would ride back and call Mum to come with the gun.

'Roo Shooting by the Dam

At night Dad would make a fire (always being aware of the wind direction and the carrying of our scent), and erect a small shelter using a couple of sheets of iron, in case it rained. This would make us less visible, so we could surprise the kangaroos as they came for water. We used the carbide light which was perfect for out in the open as well as made us less conspicuous. The kangaroos would travel at night and end up around a dam or waterhole to camp. Dad had a spot light and would take a shot when possible. At day break we would go and search for the dead or wounded animals; Dad would skin them, roll the hides up to keep them soft and moist, then head back to camp to peg them out on the ground (using cut wire as nails). In wet weather the skins would be pegged on the large gum trees to dry out. Sometimes it was necessary to roll the skins in coarse salt to stop them from rotting, especially if they could not be dried. These were the type of jobs that men took on after the War was over as money was scarce and jobs were hard to find.

My main chores during the day, as a kid, was to keep an eye on the skins drying, as the goannas liked to rip them up off the ground and spoil the skins. My bike came in handy for checking if the skins were safe. Mum would come with the gun if I warned her of the predators.

Dad would borrow a saddle horse from the local cattle station to use when he was setting snares along the dividing fences within the cattle property to catch the kangaroos as they dug through the fence. Usually, the kangaroos would get caught by the leg. The property owners were always helpful as they were keen to get rid of the 'roos since they were destroying the grass, which was essential feed for the cattle.

Other afternoons, if the wind was right, as the 'roos started to move, Mum would drive the T-Model Ford Ute with Dad standing in the back with the gun, and me sitting or standing too as we would try to spot 'roos on the plains. As soon as we spotted a 'roo we would tap the hood of the car so Mum would stop and we would all be very quiet, so Dad could take an accurate aim, before the mob dispersed into the sunset.

Setting up Camp

We moved camp about three times. Our beds were homemade, using pieces of galvanized pipe for the frame with a strong canvas base. Saplings were cut to form legs for tables, etc.

The Model T Ford utility tray at the back was for carrying our tent, poles, and accessories for setting up a temporary place to keep safe and dry. Plus, the skins had to be transported back to market. My bike ended up on top of the load.

Primary School — Kalpowar State School

Grade 4

The family relocated to Kalpowar, about 40 miles away, on the Monto/Gladstone Road; Kalpowar had a Post Office Store, Petrol Bowser, School, Butcher shop, and Forestry Office. We lived at my Aunt Doll and Uncles Stans in a large shed for a year, that Dad fixed up to make liveable. See Ludlow's Farm for more details.

Grade 5

This was the year that girls learned how to sew and once a week the principal's wife would take sewing classes, and we each worked on producing a sewing sample on a long piece of cloth. It was basic stitches, e.g. hemming, button hole, back stitch, darning, sewing on buttons and, fancywork stitches, e.g. stem stitch, blanket stitch, satin stitch, etc.

Grade 6

School projects were things like Milk and Cream Testing (measuring the butterfat in the cow's milk), Pine trees (learning their botanical names), Poultry (identifying the various breeds of fowls).

The school principal elected me to give a lecture about a cow at this special presentation. A cow was tied to the fence with a short rope, and students and parents stood around, and I felt a bit nervous about remembering my presentation. While I am concentrating, and trying to follow the cow as she moved, it was not easy to directly point my finger to various parts of the cow's body, e.g. brisket, udder, hooves. The cow kept moving around, as she was feeling nervous and worried, and the next minute she did a big "dollop" (cow pad) right there as I was concentrating, and of course I stepped in it. I am sure that put me off my project subject somewhat. "A Power-Pat-Presentation" you could call it for sure!

School lunch time

I usually rode my bike home from school for lunch; that was possible as we lived closer to the school now, and not too far from the post office, often collecting our mail on the way. I would ride my bike full pelt down the hill from school, over the railway line, and then a quick bend around the corner to the home stretch. This day I am flying down the hill, and lifted my bottom off the seat as the wheels went over the railway line, turned to follow the road and went sliding sideways on my bike into the gravel. There are still scars on my elbows from the busters off my bike. Sometimes, I would collect the mail and bread, place them in my arm while pedalling home, and steering with my arms full. "Look, no hands" and crash! My middle toe still has a bump on it as evidence of that overconfidence, as my foot slipped off the bike pedal and speared into the road.

Baked fish

One geography lesson at school inspired me and my class mate Gwenda Dunn; we decided to make an afternoon free to give the baked fish idea a try, just as was described in the school lesson. The plan was to dig some worms, go to the creek, catch a fish, bake it in hot coals, and then eat our dinner at the creek bed. Off we set on foot with a sugar bag, knife, jam tin full of worms, two fishing lines, and a box of matches. Luckily, we got a few bites, and managed to catch two perch. We dug a hole in the sand, made a fire in the hole to make hot coals, mixed up some mud (dirt/clay mixed with water), caked it onto the fish, and when the fire was turning to coals, threw in the whole fish to cook. It was a bit of a messy job really. It was exciting for us to do this new thing, as we were not sure if it would work and if we could eat our catch. Yes, we attempted to eat it and we didn't get sick, but it was a bit yuk, pulling the baked clay/mud off the fish 'cos out came the "innards" and all, then we proceeded to pick out the cooked flesh to eat. We only did this, just once, and felt satisfied we knew how to survive in the bush!

Grade 7 — Scholarship Year

1951: This was a big year, and to pass Scholarship was important for entry into the work force or Secondary school. The poor Principal had a school of 50 students and 6 of them were due to sit for their Scholarship exam, including me. Everybody got through it, and that was a miracle. The Education Department had transferred this really good Teacher, Jack Heber, to the school the year previous and he did a mighty job to get everybody up to par.

The Kalpowar Primary School was closed in 1997 with only five pupils remaining.

1950
OUR OWN HOUSE NEAR THE TENNIS COURT

The family bought a small house, in the small town of Kalpowar.

Ultimately, Dad and his father pulled the iron off the sides and replaced it with weatherboards. It was a good spot and close to the railway siding and main road, sports oval and tennis court. I was able to walk to school or ride my bike. The school was right up on top of the hill looking over the town (by the way this town only had about 40 houses). My Uncle Arthur Hansen and Aunt Claude lived just 300 yards away so we kids would scoot from one house to the other.

Our new house was situated a couple of creek crossings from my Aunt Doll and Uncle Stan's farm and I would commute by horse or bike at the weekends, and often they would call in as they went to collect groceries or mail. I now realise that was an important connection for me as family always made us welcome as kids.

Cooking — Wood Stove

Our small cottage had a wood fired stove which was during the days before power was available. Dad's first job in the morning (usually about daybreak) was to fire up the stove as it would take about half an hour before the kettle would be boiled and ready to make a cuppa-tea. With cold water in winter, the early face wash was a wake-up call. This is a photo of a stove similar to ours. Dry wood would be stacked in the wood box next to the stove. The wood box had to be filled up every evening, as well as wood chips for starters, ready for firing up the stove each morning. The stove stayed alight all day as it would be used to boil the kettle, heat the bath water, and warm up the house in cold weather.

Water

Water was supplied by catching rain water from the roof and diverting it into a tank. Water was very scarce for drinking and washing and was collected from all roof tops. Each shed, cow yard or building, had a small tank for convenience for washing, rinsing, bathing, cleaning things like the separator and buckets from the small dairy (one or two cows).

Bathing in Winter

As time went on, we got upgrades to the stove and when we got a model with a water gin on the side with a tap that was real progress. In fact, I think Dad made this water gin out of galvanised iron and fitted it to the side of the fire box. Imagine as a kid, getting in a small round tub positioned near the stove to have a bath sitting in two inches of water — damn cold in winter! It was more like armpits and crotch; often during winter I would try to get out of having a bath, as it was so cold. Besides, our air conditioning was cracks in the doors, and with no lining on the walls, that meant at each bath I had goosebumps!

Furnishings of Our House

Each bedroom had a double bed. The main bedroom had a double wardrobe and duchess, and the two other rooms had a piece of furniture as seen in the picture. The lounge housed a linen cupboard, sewing machine, ironing board, and writing desk. The kitchen had a bench for meal preparation, with a large tin dish for washing the dishes.

The kitchen table had six chairs, and was the only table in the house.

Sewing

Google reports:

> *The Wertheim Sewing Machine Company was founded in 1868 by Joseph Wertheim (1804–1899) in Frankfurt, Germany. While these treadle machines don't have the wide variety of stitch options, or the computerised features, in many ways they outshone their modern counterparts. Here are some reasons modern sewers choose vintage machines: Durability — Vintage sewing machines are made well.*

The Wertheim treadle sewing machine was popular, and reliable, and went by pedal power which made it economical and versatile. Most women/mothers mended and/or made their children's clothes. It was tricky to mend trouser legs and many wives did hand sewing, using a needle and thread. My Mum had a Wertheim Treadle Sewing Machine and made all of my school uniforms for boarding school. I was allowed to use this machine to sew bloomers to be worn under the school uniform. Nothing was wasted. Trousers would be patched front and back. Old trousers were cut up to make the patches for other trousers and finally they would be used as rags, foot rags, oily rags, mats, etc.

1948 — A New Baby

My brother Keron was born when I was ten, and this put more pressure on the jobs to be done after school, especially since Dad had a job snigging logs at Mullet Creek, several miles over the range, and would come home at weekends. There was always one or two cows to milk, as well as separating the milk, feed the chooks, fill the wood box, shake the cream for butter, feed the poddy calf, water the goat, etc. We supplied some milk to the local families. Times were tough; we separated the milk to get enough cream to make butter. We had chooks for eggs and poultry. Dad grew veggies and Mum grew flowers. If you could not eat it, Dad would not grow it!

Mullet Creek Hoop Pine Forest

The Animals

Billy Goat

Our new house was not such a great location for Billy since he had more freedom at the farm, and he never got restrained. He was part of the family and came with us, and unfortunately life was not so free and easy and he was not used to boundaries, and was tied with a long leash, and moved regularly from post to post. That was not a good thing, and I was not used to taking care of him on a daily basis.

My Dad made a cart as well as harness and bridle to fit Billy (see the Arnott's Biscuit Ad on the Box Trailer)! In this photo I am driving Billy with my sister Fay and cousin Dawn Ludlow on board.

Billy Goat Stories

I got Billy as a pet when we lived at Howie's farm. He was my mate. One night he slept on the hood of the T-Model Ford and his hoof went through the canvas. Dad opened the back door at about 5am this morning and he saw the goat's leg hanging through the hood of the car — well, emotion woke everybody. Billy was in trouble.

Another afternoon as I was walking to the cow yard Billy was playing a game and tried to follow my pathway on the track, and he galloped along the same track as me, and he was going fast, just clipped my knee, and I stumbled, just enough for his horn to put a cut on my cheek. So poor old Billy was in more strife — Dad got the hack-saw and cut off his horns to about 3 inches long (just above the tender spot). Being an only child, at this stage, the animals were my family I guess and Billy did not mean to cause any trouble, but just surprise me!

Creamy Pony

Creamy was my very own pony (Creamy in colour), hence his name Creamy. This incident was scary, but exciting when Creamy, that Pa gave to me when he was born, was being broken-in (tamed to be ridden) came out of the crush with his tackling on (harness) in such a hurry he hit the split-log fence rails with such force he dislocated his neck. Unfortunately, Creamy had to be put out to the spelling paddock before the job of breaking him in could be continued. He was a bit of a rogue. His Mum ran wild in the paddock with other horses until he was born.

Unless animals are pets, and see humans regularly, there is a lot more repetition in the preparation of the horse and, in Creamy's case required constant handling to gain confidence in the handler/rider and humans. Wild animals do not like being constrained with bridles, shin pads, halters, etc. Once the tackling goes over its back and the girth is tightened under the belly the anxiety for the animal will most likely go to another level, and it may start snorting, prancing and fidgeting around.

Fortunately, my dad always came to the rescue when there were jobs to be done. He trained and replaced horse shoes and could put his mind to almost anything that needed doing in the bush. Being multi-skilled was a definite advantage.

Years later, all of my siblings got the pleasure of looking after Creamy while I went to Boarding School, and then left home to work in the city. Creamy stayed in our family for 30 years until he had a "turn", came up to my Mum, rubbed his nose and head on her arm and keeled over dead. Tears came to my eyes when Mum told me this. The story still makes me feel sad.

The young Joey in the photo was reared from a baby, and we all loved looking after them. At bedtime the young 'Roos liked jumping head first into a sleeve of an old woollen jumper; it must have resembled the comfort of the mother's pouch.

Tennis

I started playing tennis often, and was always ready for a hit once I finished my after-school jobs. The court was made of ant bed and often had heaps of weeds. Our house was in a good spot and I would sit on the steps and either watch tennis or cricket matches while pretending I was doing my homework. Yes, I was no scholar!

Jobs Before and After School

This is not my photo; however, it really shows what I am describing about milking the house cow.

Milking our pet cow/cows daily was to be done rain hail or shine. This photo will give an idea of what the job entailed. Our pet cow Hoppy would stand in the gully or under a tree for me to milk her. There was no rope tied to the cow's leg, as I would approach "Hoppy" slowly and quietly and she was patient until the job was done. Then, it was a short bike ride home with half-a-bucket of milk in one hand, steering the bike with the other. This gave the family enough milk, cream and butter for meals, as well as enough milk/cream for cooking cakes and puddings. I could usually coax the milking cow to stand in the paddock and be milked. Fortunately, by handling the animals daily they got quiet and

usually cooperated, particularly if I handed them a treat to munch on while milking! Milking daily was imperative as that is where the milk, butter and cream came from for our meals, as well as supplying a few of the local families with a billy of fresh milk.

After milking was done, the milk had to be separated, which meant each spout had its job to do (cream down one spout, and separated milk down the other). This was so the family could have butter and cream for the lunches, and meals. The separated milk was for the poddy's dinner.

A small hand turned separator

Wood Box to fill and Chooks to Feed

Other daily jobs to be done after school, without fail. There were chooks to feed, eggs to be collected and the chook pen to be locked to keep out the predators.

This photo shows Dad and his brother Arthur having a yarn at the wood heap while splitting wood.

Social Life

It was always exciting when the Orchestra would travel to play for district dances and balls. My Uncle Alf (Violin) and Uncle Bill (Saxophone) and Aunt Cass (piano) were the main musicians. Pommer, who has the smoke in his mouth loved a beer, and by the end of the night he would get into "top gear" and sway with the beat of the drums, and as he worked those drum sticks, he would swipe the drum stick across his throat making a strange sound with his tongue. At one of the venues for Saturday night dances the stage for the musicians was in a corner with galvanised iron sides, and Pommer the drummer, would pull his drum sticks across the tin making other musical noises. At interval (a break in between the dances or at supper time), we kids would slide around the dance floor pulling each other. Many a sprained wrist was had from squatting, and being pulled, and down we would go straight on our bottoms. The floors were so slippery sprinkled with sawdust and kerosene.

The dances and music were really old time with a waltz, fox trot, progressive barn dance, gipsy tap, with music *How Much is that Doggie in the Window* by Patti Page, *It's a long way to Tipperary* by Nathan Lay, *Over the Rainbow* by Louis Armstrong, *The Road to Gundagai* by Banjo Patterson, *You are my Sunshine* by Jimmy Davis; *Auld Lang Syne* was sung with arms linked in a huge circle as a finale. We girls, and young women, would joke about the senior guy referred to as "the wandering hand society" who would love grabbing us young females to dance and swing us off our feet, and holding us as close as possible to his body. Well, my young cousin asked, "Did he have a wooden leg?" and that cracked me up!! Yes, he would stamp his foot and it would echo off the galvanised walls, and wooden floors. These dance stories are getting better as I remember other things we did at the dances, especially when the orchestra would want a break. Hokey Pokey with actions, would be sung while we all joined a large circle. Bunny Hop, was also fun where those who wanted to join into a long line holding each other's waistline. I can hear the chorus in my mind right now:

> *Can your mother ride a bike in the middle of the night,*
> *with her legs tied tight to the handle bars…*

Another lyric:

> *There are rats, rats, as big as Tom cats,*
> *In the store, in the store.*
> *There are rats, rats, as big as Tom cats,*
> *At the Quartermaster's store.*
>
> *My eyes are dim, I cannot see*
> *I have not brought my specs with me …*

We kids had a great time, and a late night too!

Fishing

Sometimes we would find jewfish nests in fresh flat creek beds with fresh running water, which would be under a shady area, near the edge of the creek, built in the shape of a ring of stones.

After a fresh in the creek (flood) Dad would get the fishing line out to try his luck out for a catch of fresh water Jew fish, and maybe perch.

There was a creek behind our house with a large waterhole, and I would go fishing with Margaret Myles my cousin. Firstly, we would dig our own worms, that lived in the damp ground under the kitchen window. The choice of catch was Jew, Perch or Eel, and occasionally a turtle would tug on the line. We liked throwing the line in a deep clear hole that you could see the hook, and see the fish coming towards the bait — that was exciting while waiting for them to get hooked. Eels were scary to catch as they had sharp teeth and would wriggle and get tangled in the line, and a sharp knife, and strong stick was part of our fishing kit, just in case we got into trouble with getting the hook out of the eel's mouth. We would try to stun the eel with the stick so we could take the hook out of its mouth without getting bitten.

1950 — A Second Brother, Noel, was Born

Unfortunately, the Doctor had grave concern for Noel's health (he may have had a hole in his heart). Dad had hired help, on Doctor's orders, to allow Mum more time to look after him. At the age of 11 months, he got a cold and developed pneumonia and died. That was sad; all the relatives came to the house, brought flowers and bits of wire, and made wreaths for his grave. I did not go to the funeral, but stayed at home to babysit my two siblings. It was not a good day for me. I felt completely alone, with no one to talk to. I could hear and see what was happening. My Mum brought some black material in Monto, and stayed up all night sewing a black dress (on the treadle sewing machine), and I woke up hearing the treadle sewing machine going, and started crying. I tossed and turned all night.

1952–1953
St Faith's Boarding School, Yeppoon
Secondary School

Boarding school had a chapel, a large building at the bottom of the hill that housed the front reception, the lounge, and the kitchen/dining area. There was a laundry behind the kitchen. There were a couple of tennis courts closer to the front entrance to the school, and a large oval on a lower level. At the top of the hill, as seen in the picture, there was a long covered-way that led to Carlton House, the boarders' dormitories. We always had a teacher on duty at night. I guess it looked like a hospital with a bed and duchess for each student.

My parents wanted us kids to have more opportunities than they had. Boarding school was the only choice as there was no local high school and no school bus runs. Naturally, being a kid, I said I did not want to go as I had no idea what it really meant and was nervous and shed a tear. Tears did not work at our house as whatever was required to happen just happened in spite of any tears, or complaints. Yes, I was scared. It turned out to be one of the great things in my life.

Dad had a plan to fund education for the kids. He leased a plot of land from the Forestry Department to be able to agist a small number of beef cattle to fatten, and raise enough funds to pay the school fees. There was not a great choice of which school; it was more about what my parents could afford. Mum made all my uniforms on a treadle sewing machine.

The first term Mum came by train to the school to enrol me and show me how to catch and change trains at the rail junctions. There were two other students, Joan Skaines (RIP) and Heather Gardiner (RIP), all dressed in uniform on the train and were heading back to school as well. I was so overawed by the whole thing by the time I got on to the train. I could not sleep all night, could not eat breakfast, talked incessantly and rushed around. I was looking out the train windows and could not sit still. The train trip took about 10 hours with loss of time changing trains at Gladstone, and Rockhampton. This opportunity to get out, meet other kids, probably shaped my adolescence, and I loved the company, activities and sport (since my life to this stage had been very isolated and sheltered). School work was always a problem as I had a memory like a sieve. Nothing much has changed except that I have become more organised. Maybe one of the things Dad would say stuck in my mind, "If you see a wise man, follow him." Even today I do look out for those clues in people I meet.

If you see a wise man, follow him.

During the First term

Unfortunately, I had gained heaps of weight, from the lack of exercise, and too much tuck shop food (dry bread and jam), and could hardly fit into my uniforms. Poor Mum had to let out every seam on every dress so it would fit without wrinkling up — the sleeves were so tight, like bands.

School Chapel

At school we attended Chapel in the morning and every evening for about half an hour. I enjoyed singing the hymns and Christmas carols. During the school holidays I would walk about singing the hymns, e.g. *All People on Earth, Abide with me, Rock of Ages*, etc.

The school routine

The school was run to schedule and a bell would ring for every command, and the new kids would wonder which direction to head when the bell rang, so I just went with the crowd. Accommodation consisted of a senior dormitory, and junior dormitory including a Nurse to put the junior school kids to bed and attend to them if they were sick. The bell would ring for every command as well, e.g., bath time, clean teeth, brush hair, sit on your bed, lights out and no talking. In the senior dormitory a Mistress would be rostered on each night to make sure it all went smoothly. We would just whisper to each other if we did not get caught. Getting caught talking or misbehaving would bring a detention, which might be to weed a garden, etc. At the end of term, before going home for the holidays, there would be a mending day scheduled where all the clothes would be folded on the bed and holes mended, and you can imagine what it was like mending socks that the toe nail had pierced. I got cunning, and cut the end of my socks off (so they were sort of three-quarter socks). This meant I did not have to face this awful task of mending holes on holes!

Sunday Church

After church, the whole senior school would be allowed to go to the beach for a swim, or a walk during winter. We would form two lines and walk for about half an hour before getting to the dressing sheds at Yeppoon beach, to get changed into our togs. After a swim the procedure would be reversed and we would get back to school for lunch.

I made some good friends at school, and in fact today maintain contact with a few of them and have attended several school reunions.

The school had mostly boarders, say 120 students, including the junior school, many of whom lived on farms and cattle stations. The students got to know each other quite well. I believe that is why so many remained friends long after boarding school.

One of the senior girls, Del Fryer was an excellent pianist, and I got this nick name "Horsey" maybe since I liked horses. Del would play this tune *Horsey Keep Ya Tail Up* and that song became a bit of a hit amongst the girls in Junior and Senior school.

My big achievement was representing the school in tennis. There were two players picked for the A team, and two for the B team, and our school would compete against other schools in the district competition on Saturdays. We would go off in the old school blunder bus in our sports gear.

The famous school bus

This is a school bus of the era of the 1940/50 because it was not a new bus. Our actual school bus had open sides, a bit like the old-style trams. There were curtains that could be drawn if it was cold or rained.

Our school bus was made with similar features, and it rattled along the road, with a driver seated at the front. Similarly, our school bus had open sides, and rows of seats that seated about 40 pupils; and was mostly used to take our school sports teams to Rockhampton for inter-school competition, e.g. tennis and netball. Every pupil would have memories of riding in the bus. My Dad always said, "A bad ride is better than a good walk," and that is the truth! The blinds at the side could be dropped down if it was cold or raining. As the bus bumped along the road our school teams would sing their House War Cries. There were three Houses (Crick, Ash and Halford named after Archbishops). Rod Laver's tennis coach (Chas Hollis, RIP) would come down to the school by train from Rockhampton about 8 times per term and coach tennis. Occasionally he would bring Rod (who was just a small freckly faced lad and subsequently became a World Tennis Champion). Chas was an excellent coach. I think his coaching ways and understanding of skills made me realise that not everyone was good at what they do. My subsequent coaching career was a very enjoyable and successful part of years of my life.

Sport has enhanced my life.

> *A bad ride is better than a good walk.*

This was the end of an era and I was then ready to get a job "somewhere". Our little village at home only had one office position, and it was not for an inexperienced school leaver. Mum had sent letters away to property owners seeking a Governess position and a person to help with the stock. It looked a bit grim, and Dad's sister Mabel Greensill and her daughter Dawn came up to our house for holidays, and Aunt Mabel agreed to bring me back to Brisbane with her and help me find an office position. I had 3 dresses, a pair of shoes, and 20 quid to help me through this period. I had no idea, and just did what I was told. The big city was not what I was used to, and I was totally lost finding my way around the Brisbane city, and had no idea what train or tram to catch. After a few weeks I got a job at DHA as an Office Assistant in the typing pool.

The rest is history, and more of that can be read at the end of this book.

1955 — Electricity Connected at Kalpowar

Power in the bush didn't happen until sometime after the larger towns and cities. Boarding school at Yeppoon with running water and power was amazing — I didn't want to leave! To finally have power in the country was such a boost as all those stirring, mixing, cutting, ironing, jobs could be done easier, providing people had the money to buy these new appliances.

Annual Leave

1955: A visit home

I had worked in Brisbane for twelve months and each holidays I would visit the family. My brother and sister (Fay and Keron) took my place when I left home to work in the city. This shows my last ride I had on a horse for a long time.

I loved my pony even though he was a bit of a rogue at times!

This photo was taken at the sports field in front of our house, and the Kalpowar Railway siding can be seen in the background.

1970s
The Modern Era

Once upon a time I did not seem to reflect on the past as much as I do today. Maybe I have gathered a lot of "dust" over the years, especially when I see opportunities clearer now, as well as attitudes that have changed, and the reluctance for young folk to "roll up their sleeves" and keep going in spite of what is thought to be "tough".

I got my first job in 1954 as a Clerical Assistant in Brisbane. It seemed to be the place of opportunity. In the country there were limited opportunities for work, sport, education, and advancement. After the first couple of years working, I had tried to take advantage of all of the opportunities. What did I do? I enrolled in shorthand classes, and sewing classes, tennis competition and tennis coaching.

I was not a scholar; but a person that kept going until I achieved improvement to move forward. This simple motto has worked for me all of my life, and I wanted to show others that they too could achieve small goals if they were consistent and persistent.

The best example of achieving goals is to look at what I have written about my ancestors, and how they worked hard, kept giving things a "go" and, in spite of adversity succeeded in rearing their families, and never gave up. Besides, these hard workers have lived a long life in spite of no handouts, a resourceful family, with a limited amount of financial assistance.

Reflections

I have got a few Myles cousins behind me now as they see me trying to put the family puzzle together; and they also have got curious as to how the lives of these pioneers came about, and why; and things like the reasons for the forebears to leave their birth country.

Margaret List (Myles) has researched into the past, and in doing so has uncovered some relative statistics that are joining up to our existing knowledge, and the puzzle is looking more complete.

We were told Mr McCord sponsored the Myles family from Scotland, and that our great grandfather David Myles (Snr) was known to him in Scotland and his knowledge as a Pioneering Teamster. David Myles Snr knew the technique of building waterproof haystacks/hay stooks and Mr McCord knew David's knowledge would be invaluable to the farming being carried out at Eidsvold and Cania Stations; July 1876 McCord and Knox from Eidsvold Station became the new owners of Cania Station.

This knowledge makes me now realise our family in Qld, as we know it today, may never have come about without Mr McCord's sponsorship.

GLOSSARY

Blacksmith	a person skilled at heating and shaping iron to make tools, brackets
Bluey	often referred to as a swag: a round bundle of clothes tied with rope, which then formed a strap to swing over the shoulder for ease of carrying
Bore	a deep hole drilled into the ground to tap into an underground water supply
Breaking in a horse	training the horse to be quiet and accept harness/saddle/bridle so humans can ride them
Branding	a method of marking stock with branding irons for identification of ownership
Bullock teams	a team of bullocks to pull heavy loads
Bushy	a person raised in the bush
Cania	a closed mining town near Cania Gorge, Qld
Clonmel State School	a one teacher school that has now closed outside of Mungungo (Upper Burnett District, Qld)
Cow bails	a structure to restrain a cow during milking
Cow crush	a narrow set of rails to confine a beast
Cow yards	a well-constructed yard that would hold a mob of cattle or horses

Cream carrier	a big lorry with driver who visited farms delivering empty cream cans, and dropping off goods, bread and mail
Cross-cut saw	a long saw with large teeth for cutting very large logs by hand
Dicky seat	seat at the back of an early model passenger car
Dipping	directing cattle into a race that leads to a swim through a trough that contained a mixture that would kill ticks
Dolly pot	a portable tool used for crushing small quantities of gold-bearing rock, by hand
Double-bank	an adult riding a horse with a pillion rider, usually a child
Draft horse	a strong stocky horse to pull heavy loads; identified by their hairy fetlocks
Dunny	lavatory
Durry	a cigarette
Epidemic	spreading of contagious illness
Feeding poddies	feeding baby calves
Gold Rush	when a lot of people rush to a place in search of precious minerals
Golembil/Barrimoon Rail Tunnels	(over great dividing range) — walks and hiking
Gramophone	a wind-up turntable to play records

Grid	prevents stock from escaping replacing a gate that divides two properties
Horse breaking	taming a horse to be ridden
Hoop pine logging	cutting timber, and hauling the product to rail or mill
Joe Blow	snake
Kalpowar State School	a school that has now closed
Leg rope	a means of restraining a cow when being milked
Lizard lips on toast	way to describe what you were going to have on your toast for breakfast
Many Peaks	a deserted mining town, in the Gladstone district of the Boyne Valley, Qld
Milking machine	apparatus attached to a cow's teat to extract milk
Monal	situated about 370km north-northwest of Brisbane. A deserted mining village, on the outskirts of Monto, Qld
Ploughing	making deep furrows in the ground to prepare a vegetable patch
Pooper Scooper	a horse/tractor drawn gadget to collect cow manure from the cow yard
Pushing scrub	clear land with a lot of trees on a mountain
Ramp	a couple of logs placed to assist loading logs onto a railway truck or semi-trailer

'Roo shooting	culling kangaroos in seasonal times; shooting kangaroos for their skins.
Separator, hand-wound	machine to separate cream from milk
Saddle	especially for horses to make a seat on their back
Snigging logs	using horses or tractor to drag logs to a ramp
Stock whip	a stockman's whip for controlling a herd
Stompers	machinery to crush rocks
Sulky	a horse drawn carriage
Trough	a sealed container that holds food/water for stock
Well	a large square hole in the ground dug to find underground water
Windlass	a hand-powered winding device for hauling dirt/stones up a shaft
Windmill	wind-driven huge fan to pump water from a bore or well into a trough or tank
Wonty-gong	something with no name
Wood box	storage for firewood in the fire place/kitchen

FOOTNOTES
Simple Phrases are Expressions

BUSH SPEAK is about what a bushy means by simple phrases.

Saying	Meaning
Got ding bats in the belfry Mad as a hatter	Mad
Screwy Silly as a two-bob watch Silly as a wheel	Silly
Works more points than a porcupine	Avoids responsibility
Cunning as a shit house rat Take the shirt off your back	Rogue
Sick in the head	Always not well
Call a spade a spade	Say what you mean
Shit on the liver	Cranky
Can't get out of your own road	Lazy
Lives on the smell of an oily rag Got your first two bob	Lousy
Stubborn as a mule	Will not change their mind
More money than sense	Extravagant
Keep it under your hat Mum's the word	Secret

Feel crook One bung lung Galloping consumption Feel sick as a dog	Sick
Got itchy feet, scratch 'em	Restless
No gumption	No common sense
Joe Blow	A snake
A soak	A drunk
Good as gold I'm as right as rain Set as a jelly	Everything is OK
Go like a bat out of hell Shake a leg Get a wriggle on	Move quickly, hurry up
Green as grass	A little naïve
It never rains but it pours	Everything happens at once
Make hay while the sun shines	Play up while you can
Were you vaccinated with a gramophone needle? Talk the leg off an iron pot Enough lip for another row of teeth	Never stops talking
You could talk under water You could talk under wet cement	Never shuts up
Chatter box Talking ten to the dozen	Talking quickly, excited

Raining cats and dogs	Pouring rain
Never rains but it pours	
Growing web feet	Very wet weather
Get your act together	Stop mucking about
Batching	Male left to look after themselves at home
Don't beat around the bush	Tell the truth
Lives like a dog in a hollow log	Hermit-style living
Wing-wong for a gooses bridle	Do not know the name of the gadget
Fit as a fiddle	Rearing to go
Don't know him from a bar of soap	Do not recognise this person
Rough as guts	Not a neat job
Could eat a horse and chase the rider	Hungry
What do you do for a crust?	What is your job/work?
Duffer	Not thinking straight
Stone the crows	Unbelievable
A stitch in time saves nine	If it is broken, fix it
The early bird catches the worm	Start early
There is only quick or dead	Move faster
Slow as Methuselah	Taking too long

Give up the ghost	Stop trying
Run off your feet Flat out like a lizard drinking Busy as a bee Busy as a dog with fleas Have not got time to scratch myself	Busy
Dressed up like a sore toe	Look lovely
All dressed up, and nowhere to go Waiting around like a stale bottle of piss	Dressed, and don't know what to do
Stone the crows	Surprised to see you
Grab the bull by the horns	Hurry up and do it
White as a sheet	Got a fright
All hands to the pump	Everyone helps please
Cool as a cucumber	In control
Stop your rot Put your foot down with a firm hand	Behave yourself
Smart Alec	Cheeky
Bashing your head against a brick wall	Getting nowhere
Thick as a brick If brains were dynamite, it would not blow the top off your hat	No brains
Cannot get a word in edge-ways You have been vaccinated with a gramophone needle	Everybody talking at once
More brains than sense	Ideas that will not work

See a wise man, follow him	Take a good pathway
A good day's work for good day's pay	Don't be lazy
You are hard to follow	Confusing
Assassinate you with a glance	Behave yourself
That is your form!	Acting in a way nobody likes
Stop bumming around!	Don't expect others to look after you
Like Father like Son	Following in your dad's footsteps
Paddle your own canoe	You are on your own
Up the creek without a paddle	Stuck
Weak as water	Could not stand up for yourself
Weak as a kitten	Not very strong
You can lead a horse to water but you cannot make it drink	You can show a person but you cannot make them do it
That's always on the cards If it does happen, I'll eat my hat	It could happen
That's a feather in your cap Your blood is worth bottling Worth your weight in coarse salt It's the bees' knees It's a bobby dazzler	You did well
Make hay while the sun shines	Keep going while things are working

Don't let the grass grow under your feet	Keep on moving — don't stand still
You think I came down in the last shower	Expecting a person to believe a lie
Steal the eye out of a needle	Take things they should not take
Birds of a feather flock together	Those who think the same stay together
Sticks and stones will break my bones and names will never hurt me	Name calling
Shut the gate after the horse has bolted	Too late acting
Slow as a wet week So slow you couldn't catch a cold Thick as a brick	Slow on the uptake
You're a mug lair	Show-off
It never rains but it pours	Everything happens at once
Rip the fork out of your nightie	Catastrophe
How long is a piece of string?	What is the limit?
Raining cats and dogs Never rains but it pours	Pouring rain
My mouth is so dry I cannot spit	Badly need a drink of water
Don't spread yourself too thin	Keep some excess
That's it in a nutshell	Something well summarised

ENDNOTE
Brief Summary of My Life

1938 Born at Cracow Qld during the gold rush.

1945–51 Primary Schools Clonmel, and Kalpowar

1952–53 St Faiths Boarding School — the highlight tennis coaching with Chas Hollis.

1954 Moved to Brisbane. Commenced working at Drug Houses of Australia as a clerical assistant.

Working life before marriage:

1955 Braemar Engineering as Junior Stenographer;

1957 PMG Telegraph Service as Junior Stenographer.

1957 PMG Engineering Typing Pool — Stenographer.

1957 Represented the Postal Institute Tennis at Interstate Sports Carnival, Perth.

1957 PMG Temporary transfer Engineering Rockhampton — Typist/Teleprinter.

1957 Attended night school at Nunn & Trivets' for 120wpm speed shorthand training.

1958 Commenced playing squash.

1959 Temporary transfer to Prime Ministers Department, Canberra — Stenographer.

1961 Bought a house at Holland Park West

1961/63 Married — Worked at Secretarial for Austral Air Conditioning; Secretarial at Electric Control and Engineering.

1963–69 Reared three sons Peter, Floyd and Jason.

1971–72–73 Represented Qld Women's squash at the national championships being part of the Australian Women's Event Winners in Perth 1973.

1974–1996 Squash Coach, Level 1, Level 2, First Aid Certificate, Massage course and Referee, Director of Coaching.

1974–84 Appointed part time Metropolitan Region Coach.

1975 Established a small business (G & R Distributors).

1979–1996 State Coaching Director.

1990 Winner of World Masters Over 50 Women's Singles, Sydney — Gold Medal.

2002–2019 Produced squashgame.info with Ray Strachan. Former Squash Australia Development Officer.

2008 Published an ebook *Reared in a Tent*

2018 Represented Australia in the O/80's World Table Tennis in Las Vegas.

2019 Published a book *Simple Steps to Success* — tips to encourage young people to have a savings plan.

2022 Awarded the Beverley Gould "Service to Juniors Award" by Squash Australia

www.ritapaulos.com

www.ingramcontent.com/pod-product-compliance
Lightning Source LLC
Chambersburg PA
CBHW082208070526
44585CB00020B/2333